the
abandoners

Begoña Gómez Urzaiz is a freelance journalist based in Barcelona. She has published worked in *El País*, *La Vanguardia*, the Spanish editions of *Vogue*, *Vanity Fair* and several others. She co-presents a podcast called *Amiga Date Cuenta* and teaches Literary Journalism on a master's programme in Universitat Autònoma de Barcelona. *The Abandoners* is her first book.

the abandoners

Begoña Gómez Urzaiz

Translated by Lizzie Davis

THE BOROUGH PRESS

The Borough Press
An imprint of HarperCollins*Publishers* Ltd
1 London Bridge Street
London SE1 9GF

www.harpercollins.co.uk

HarperCollins*Publishers*
Harper Ireland
Macken House,
39/40 Mayor Street Upper,
Dublin 1
D01 C9W8

First published in Great Britain by HarperCollins*Publishers* 2024

1

A catalogue record for this book is available from the British Library

Hardback ISBN: 9780008656072

Set in Adobe Garamond by Palimpsest Book Production Limited,
Falkirk, Stirlingshire

Printed and bound in the UK using 100% Renewable Electricity at
CPI Group (UK) Ltd

For my mother, who is always there.
And for Ciarán, Lope, and Sean: I want you close always.

Contents

'It is well known in the world of fairy-tale and post-Freudian analysis that it is not a good thing for a child to have a wicked witch, especially a lovely wicked witch, as a mother'

Jenny Diski, 'Entitlement', *LRB*

What Kind of Mother Abandons Her Child?

There's something biblical to the phrase, and it arrives in the mouth fully formed, a little like: 'Who could kill a child?' It has that judgemental feel, slightly self-righteous, like all words that dress up as common sense, that boast of being free of ideology. Everyone knows when someone invokes common sense, they're trying to get you to vote conservative.

Even so, almost no one has escaped articulating it on some occasion, upon hearing or reading about a woman who, at a certain point, left her children behind and carried on with her non-mother life. 'A child will change your life' is another one of those phrases, persistent and posed like an incontrovertible fact. If they change your life, it can't be unchanged. That's ontologically impossible: the child can't be undone.

What kind of mother abandons her child? The worst kind, certainly.

The question has seized me many times: I'd swear it's against my will, as if I'm possessed by a moralist I don't believe myself to be, or a kind of moralist that makes me uncomfortable.

It happened, for example, the day I went to see *Carol*, the Todd Haynes film based on the Patricia Highsmith novel *The Price of Salt*. It was a special day, my eldest son's second birthday, so I remember the exact date. It had been an exhausting weekend of maternal-affective overproduction. That Saturday, I had invited the family over for dinner, cooked for nine, and we blew out candles. On Sunday, the idea was to do something simple, with friends, at the park. Everyone knows how that turns out. I woke up very early to make pastrami sandwiches and tuna empanadas and carry them to the picnic tables, along with drinks, snacks, a garland, candles, balloons, plates, a piñata, a big tin of potato crisps – the fancy kind – and cups from Flying Tiger. Luckily, a lot of people came. It was nice, and tiring. A friend brought a strawberry cream cake so photogenic it seemed like it was straight out of an insurance ad. The perfect metonym for 'happy moments for you and yours'. Everyone brought gifts, though we had told them it wasn't necessary. When my phone highlights photos of that day, something the 'For You' feature does from time to time, exerting a subtle form of emotional terrorism, it moves me just as Apple hopes it will. I shudder in my motherhood.

When I see a photo of that children's party, or any of the others I've now thrown, all that comes to mind is noise, happiness, sunshine, the crocodile piñata. Not the anxiety of preparing it all, the stress of spending so much, the supreme fatigue that locks all my muscles the moment I've collected the last streamer, thrown out the last paper cup with dinosaurs on it.

At the end of that particular afternoon, I felt like I had spent time with everyone but my child, socialising, exchanging pleasantries for five minutes while checking that there was ice enough in the cooler. Later, the party continued in our home. Regardless, when some friends of mine – without children – proposed we go to the cinema to see *Carol*, I was first to sign up. Because I wanted to see it – it had been out for two or three weeks, I felt like the only person who hadn't yet, and thus was excluded from the conversation – and because at that time, I was still performing an idea for myself: that you can do it all, be it all, and be all right. Stay current with what's on at theatres, provide tireless care, turn in eight articles a week, aim for at least three that wouldn't leave me shamefaced if I came across them on the internet months later.

The point is, I went to the theatre to see *Carol*, and I didn't like it as much as I thought I would. Partly because it was hard for me to buy Todd Haynes's style; partly because I was tired and felt a needling of guilt (nothing too serious, medium-low intensity guilt) for not being at home with my son, watching cartoons, the two of us cuddled up after a very exhausting weekend. But most of all – and this I identified later – because of the end of the movie, which left me with a feeling that was sticky and unpleasant.

Exactly as Patricia Highsmith wrote it, Carol ends up abandoning her husband and daughter in order to live as a lesbian with some degree of peace. Her husband, a despicable person, has blackmailed her, leaving her with no choice. Either she relinquishes the girl, or she lives out the rest of her life unhappy, denying her authentic desire, lying to herself and everyone else.

The options are clear, aren't they? The film reflects no ambivalence whatsoever on the part of Carol/Cate Blanchett. That's strange coming from an author so accustomed to exposing the dustiest corners of the human mind, especially one whose relationship with her own mother was hyper-pathological (the mother often recounted how she had tried to abort her by drinking turpentine). It would be understandable for Carol to feel a certain resistance to the daughter who represents her ties to the world of the husband, as sometimes happens when a child becomes identified with the relationship that created her. But that's not what happens in the book. Carol adores her daughter, whom she will never see again. In Haynes's film, we see the girl, Rindy, on a couple of occasions. In the novel, there's no need even for that. Rindy is not a real person, she's an abstraction: the platonic ideal of a little girl, wearing pigtails and a jumper. The film is constructed so the modern viewer, who is presumably in favour of the original work, doesn't have to give the matter too much thought. Yes, there's a trace of bitterness to the ending, but it's also the only one possible.

Why, then, had it made me so uncomfortable? Why did my mind arrive at a place where I asked Carol again and again how she had been capable of giving up her daughter? Wasn't the answer obvious? It was the only decision that would allow her to live.

I was still asking myself years later, when everyone was celebrating Patricia Highsmith's centenary, and more or less the same sentence appeared in each article on the subject: '*The Price of Salt* was the first lesbian novel with a happy ending.' That's what the author herself had said in the prologue and epilogue of the novel when it was reissued years later, by then a contemporary classic, and almost all the news outlets repeated it. But what do you mean happy, I blurted out every time I read that, a guest on my very own talk-show. If she never sees her daughter again. How can that ending be happy.

I identified that it wasn't the first time that judgemental spring had gone off in me, the spring that upsets and repels me, that simply doesn't fit with the fourth-wave feminism I practise and preach daily in articles, tweets, and conversations. My generation arrived late to feminism, but we've compensated for that with the most ardent evangelising. Wherever we go, we offer anti-misogynistic sermons for anyone who wants to listen, and also for those who don't.

Digging around, I realise that gauge, the dubious-mother detector, took hold of me even as a teenager, when I first read

Anna Karenina and reproached Tolstoy for not having written more about Seryozha, the son Anna leaves behind when she chooses to go off with Vronsky. Now it strikes me as odd that even at sixteen years old, I was already more concerned with the fate of the child than with how oppressive Anna's fate would be if she continued to be married to Karenin. What a waste of the adolescent mind, I think now, what a germ of a petite-bourgeoisie philosopher.

My invisible list of negligent mothers, part- or full-time, continued to grow over the years, like a registry where I noted each case I came across without giving it much thought. Ingrid Bergman. Gala Dalí. Maria Montessori. Muriel Spark. Mercè Rodoreda. Doris Lessing. Anna Akhmatova. Susan Sontag. I don't believe in the separation between an artist and her work. I'm very interested in the lives of the people I read and whose work I follow, but this seemed to go a bit beyond standard curiosity. It was as if I were compiling an inquiry file on mothers who had neglected their duties, a mental folder titled The Abandoners.

I had started maintaining it early, the folder. As a child, I often watched the series *Pippi Longstocking*, which they showed on Saturday mornings on Televisión Española. I loved the saturated sixties colours, the flower-covered streets of that Swedish town where the sun was always out, and so was Pippi. But the show also made me feel somewhat unsettled. Where were Pippi's parents? It was great that they'd left her alone in Villa Villekulla with a trunk full of gold coins, but why wasn't anyone there to make her an omelette at dinnertime? When neighbourhood children Tommy and Annika ask if she wants to come live with them and their parents – a vigorous Nordic family, if a bit snobbish – it doesn't seem like a bad idea. Probably, Pippi would have to give up her monkey and her horse, relinquish all her freedom and everything that makes her unique, but in exchange, she would win normal parents and a mountain of wooden toys and mustard-coloured turtlenecks, always clean and ready in her drawer.

Now, I realise this understanding of Pippi's story is just the opposite of what its author intended, not at all the interpretation the world would expect of a child. Those stories are a celebration of childhood anarchy, creativity, and free will. What kind of girl would go and read everything backwards? A repressed one, cut out to be a traditionalist? Besides, the stories of Pippi Longstocking are inscribed within the limitless tradition of fairy tales featuring motherless children, children who have experiences. Adventure, Sara Ruddick suggests in the book *Maternal Thinking*, is an idea that's essentially free of mothers. A mother, in the end, is there to prevent bad things from befalling her offspring, and, along the way, maybe good ones too.

As a child, watching Pippi on TV, I didn't know the creator of the character, Astrid Lindgren, had become a single mother at age eighteen, following a relationship with the head of the newspaper where she worked as a stenographer. Her lover was thirty years older than her and was married. Astrid, who had hardly any money, had to leave her son, Lars, with a foster family in Denmark for three years. The author often likened that period, in which she lived alone in Stockholm without her son, to a passage through hell. If she was able to scrape together enough money, she slipped away to Copenhagen to see Lars, and when she finally managed to recover guardianship and custody, she swapped out the guilt she had felt over abandoning her child for the guilt over uprooting him from that more stable family, so much like Tommy and Annika's, who had also loved and cared for the child.

To be a mother, in the end, is to accumulate collections of

guilt that are heedless of contradicting themselves. In the universe of mothers, the guilt over temporarily leaving a child is perfectly compatible with the guilt of getting him back. All of Lindgren's work is full of parentless children, children who invent alternate biographies to explain away those absences, like Pippi herself, who tells everyone her mother is an angel and her father a shipwrecked pirate.

Nor do parents often appear in the Enid Blyton boarding-school books I devoured as a child, those racist, classist, yet completely irresistible artifacts; although in that case, the parental absence is socially acceptable, since the families have enough money to subsidise care of their children, as has happened worldwide throughout history.

The families of Darrell Rivers, the protagonist of the series *Malory Towers*, or the twins Patricia and Isabel O'Sullivan, students at St Clare's, would leave the children at the platform of the train that took them to school at the beginning of every book, and at the most, they reappeared in the final chapter to collect them. Ignorant at that point of the British class system and its educational particularities, I always wondered about those absent parents, and how it could be that their daughters willingly went off to a school in Cornwall to play lacrosse and have late-night parties with Nestlé milk and tinned sardines, in exchange for never seeing their families. Tinned sardines and a freezing pool in exchange for a mother? In truth, the twins didn't seem like the winners in that scenario, not to me.

Malory Towers, the boarding school where Blyton set the six original novels in the series, is based on Benenden School, where the author sent her own children thanks to the fortune she'd made on her children's books. Blyton had two daughters, Gillian and Imogen. They appeared in the press a few times when they were young, photographed alongside their very famous mother, petting the dogs and playing in the garden at the family home.

As adults, the two sisters didn't speak to each other, and each time they conceded interviews to their mother's biographers, they offered completely contradictory versions of what happened in their childhood and what their mother was like.

The elder of the daughters, Gillian, who was a schoolteacher and lived in a house full of Enid Blyton memorabilia, taking her afternoon tea at the very table where Blyton wrote *The Famous Five* and *The Secret Seven*, always maintained that they had a wonderful mother. The younger daughter wrote in her memoir *A Childhood at Green Hedges* that Blyton was 'arrogant, insecure, pretentious, very skilled at putting difficult or unpleasant things out of her mind, and without a trace of maternal instinct'. 'As a child,' Imogen added, 'I viewed her as a rather strict authority. As an adult, I did not hate her. I pitied her.'

It so happens that both Enid Blyton and her daughters lost contact with their biological fathers. The author's father, a cutlery salesman in Sheffield – the woman who did the most to perpetuate the British upper-class parenting style wasn't born into that world, she carved a place for herself within it by writing about the class she wished she belonged to – abandoned the family when she was a young girl, and her mother forced her to lie to the neighbours about it. Many years later, Blyton's first husband, Hugh, also fled the scene, and her daughters lost contact with their father.

The experience of losing a father not because he has died but rather because he disappears into a new life that is incompatible with his old one, as happened first to Enid then to Gillian and Imogen, falls within the category of ordinary. Fathers vanish all the time, all over the place. As a biographical data point, it's a three or four out of ten on the scale of events that shape a person's life. More significant than suffering a long childhood illness, but less so than living through a major financial crisis. Under almost no circumstance is the abandonment of a father considered comparable to the abandonment of a mother. One might expect a father to leave, but a mother, never. We say it's 'unnatural', but it isn't, because nature is full of bad mothers and mothers who leave. Seals abandon their pups. Cuckoos lay their eggs in other birds' nests and fly off. That's how they trick other mothers into caring for their chicks. There are hundreds of animal species for whom it is normal or customary to eat their own young.

Human mothers also sometimes leave. It has happened throughout time, and it still does, for all sorts of reasons. The majority of women who leave their children do so out of pure necessity, to go somewhere else and earn money, often caring for the children of others, or fleeing geopolitical devastation. Some of these women were generous enough to share their stories with me, and they appear in the second-to-last section of this document, which I didn't call a book for a very long time.

There are also women, fewer, who relinquish custody of their children the moment they're born. It's not a crime, and it's done anonymously. The medical staff are practised and know that in this type of delivery, protocol directs they must quickly remove the baby to avoid contact with the mother. They transfer the mother to another floor so she won't hear the babies crying, nor see the halls filled with orchids. In maternity wards, they recommend taking the plants out of patients' rooms at night, to maximise the oxygen available for the new-borns. I've always been intrigued by that competition between delicate living beings.

It's easy to instinctively understand this as a kind of tragedy, and we classify it as one more element in the grand buffet of atrocities turbocapitalism produces. We might even fictionalise it mentally, with the help of all the novels we've been encountering since we were children, rich in mothers who give up their little ones and fasten delicate chains around their necks so as to recognise them twenty-five chapters later.

Go one rung up on the hierarchy of needs and the whole thing gets morally hazier. We agree we can accept leaving a child to avoid condemning him to poverty, or leaving a child to make a life in another country when that's the only available option, but leaving a child to escape an unhappy marriage? 'How unhappy? Was it violent?' the moral prosecutor inside us begins to ask. What about leaving behind a child to embrace your own sexuality, as happens in *Carol*? Or leaving behind individual care of children and collectivising it, as women do, for example, in the kibbutzim of Israel, as a precondition for communal utopia? Leaving behind a daughter to move to another country and experience volcanic love, as Ingrid Bergman did? Leaving behind a child in order to write, like Muriel Spark, Doris Lessing, or Mercè Rodoreda? Leaving behind a daughter for unknown reasons, like Gala Dalí?

Already, we're flooded with doubts, and we run the risk of finding ourselves – like I did as what I'd now call a 'pro-establishment child' – issuing rather repellent moral judgements.

One of my intentions in writing this, which strictly speaking and according to the rules of modern writing, I am not entirely authorised to write – I'll tell you now that my parents didn't abandon me, nor have I abandoned my children; I'm merely a spy in this calamity – is to ask myself where I came by that urge to condemn. Why it's so hard for me to accept that someone might want to separate from her children, for a while or forever, if I think of myself as such a devoted feminist, if I believe I have a proper understanding of human complexity and empathise with so many deviations from the norm.

Writing *The Abandoners* allowed me to spend some time exploring that mental folder, which has become something else entirely. I tried to understand the *whys* of these real and fictional women, as well as their *whens* and their *hows*. I also wanted to think about why there's still so much fear around the idea of a mother who, for a time, wants to act like she isn't one. I've tried to be generous and open-minded in responding to the question that still chases me: what kind of mother abandons her child?

Muriel Spark: A (Male) Writer's Life

The best way to lead a writer's life has been well tested and amply documented throughout history: marry a writer's wife. Nothing frees up the time and mental space required to devote oneself to filling pages like cohabitating with someone who will take care of every mundanity, including the minor detail of breadwinning, as Mercedes Barcha did when Gabriel García Márquez left journalism to concentrate on his novels. From Patricia Llosa, who so deftly packed Mario Vargas Llosa's suitcases, to Vera Nabokov, paradigm of proofreader/editor/coach/manager/agent who even licked stamps for Vladimir's letters, there's an abundant catalogue of devoted literary spouses. John le Carré's wife typed up his novels for him, and as she did, she edited and refined them. An unbeatable two for one.

In the recent history of literature, the person who came closest to obtaining an arrangement that efficient was Muriel Spark. The hyper-prolific author of *The Prime of Miss Jean Brodie*, who wrote more than twenty novels as well as many volumes of poetry, essay, memoir, and biography, spent the last thirty years of her life, when she had already achieved success and money, with an assistant and companion, Penelope Jardine, in an old converted church in Oliveto, Tuscany.

Spark had always had men as lovers, and a husband. And

Penelope and Muriel always denied that theirs was a romantic relationship, or a kind of Boston marriage, an archaic, sotto-voce lesbian arrangement. They maintained that they simply had a satisfactory domestic situation. Whether or not they were sleeping together, Jardine performed, with near Nabokovian mastery (Vera's, of course) the role of the writer's wife, diligently managing a portfolio of household and administrative tasks that ranged from talking with agents to overseeing translation contracts, accepting or rejecting invitations to literary festivals, booking plane tickets, and driving the old BMW when the two of them went on holiday across Europe. Muriel always sat in the passenger's seat and occupied herself pulling nips of cognac from the glove compartment. There's no evidence that Jardine received compensation for any of these tasks. That's the good thing about spouses: they don't charge.

Spark is considered one of the great converts of British literature, a Jew by birth who embraced Catholicism, like her friends and benefactors Evelyn Waugh and Graham Greene. But maybe the most significant conversion she experienced in her life had less to do with religion and more to do with gender roles. With much effort and tenacity, Muriel Spark managed to write in a way that normally only men could. In order for that to be possible, two things had to happen: she needed to find that steadfast, efficient companion – Penelope – and also outsource the care of her only son, Robin.

When she died in 2006, the writer made clear in her will that none of her material assets were to go to Robin, who was still alive and a painter in Edinburgh. The press seized that detail and covered it gleefully, because a son disinherited in favour of a same-sex companion – Jardine is still the executor of Spark's literary estate – provides an interesting pulpy angle. But for those familiar with the life of the author and her family, there was little surprise in it. It was only the final chapter of a painful separation that had begun long before, in a time (the end of the 1930s) and place (Southern Rhodesia, now Zimbabwe) so distant they seem to belong to another life, another novel.

In 1939, with the Second World War underway, Muriel Spark separated de facto from her husband, left her four-year-old child in the care of nuns at a Catholic convent in the city then known as Gwelo, and embarked on a long and perilous journey to her birth city, Edinburgh. It would be more than two years before mother and son reunited, but they would never again live together. The child was raised by his grandparents, to whom Spark sent money monthly to cover his living expenses.

I started to read about Muriel Spark so I could review one of her books, which had been reissued. Then I learned about the unusual relationship she had with her son, Robin, and I couldn't help but get waylaid by that part of her biography, which some would consider minor and which had nothing to do with the book I was going to write about. There are several paths to the conclusion that her relationship with her only son is irrelevant, surfacing from several schools of thought. It could either reflect an entirely patriarchal line of thinking – 'Who cares about something like children?' – or a kind of feminist vindication, albeit slightly maternophobic – 'Spark was much more than a mother,' etc.

I've opted out of both schools. I've always wanted to know what the people who interest me do with their lives and their bodies. And I don't understand a feminism that doesn't encompass the maternal.

At that point, I had two children who were close to Robin's age when he was separated from his mother. One a little younger, the other a little older. And the idea of leaving them alone in a convent, in the care of strangers, on another continent with

14

an international conflict underway, struck me as both delusional and slightly monstrous.

On the other hand, I was four months into pandemic isolation, in a flat in Barcelona with my partner and my children, trying, among other things, to give shape to a book and balance that with the dozens of articles I publish every month (Spark, who was fantastic at managing her career, talked about that: nothing incentivises writing like the need to get paid for what you write). There were moments, about thirty-seven each day, when the possibility of being alone for a while, dedicating sixty uninterrupted minutes to working in a state of maximum concentration, seemed unattainable. Actually, it was. As anyone who has cared for small children is aware, you're living in a state of perpetual attack. Whatever is happening in your head will be swarmed and plundered at any moment, and the knowledge that this siege is imminent turns thinking, getting lost in thought, into a furtive activity.

During the day, the challenge of managing time brought me to frustrated tears, and at night, it kept me up, thinking about all the sections disappearing from the newspapers I write for, the collaborations that had been called off, my shrinking rates, the book they had commissioned from me, now at a standstill, which I would have to write tomorrow, during the brief period when the little one was napping and his brother was doing puzzles. Oh yes, in that one hour, I would be so very productive.

'At least the kids are all right,' we were constantly writing in mum group chats. 'We're doing our best,' we repeated. 'We're where we need to be.'

We had a quite limited range of set phrases at our disposal, and we passed them back and forth. The words seemed increasingly threadbare, increasingly worn out, like the typical sweater that goes from cousin to cousin in a family until the elbows are transparent and the cuffs have stretched out.

There was a residual truth to the things we said, I suppose. But the feeling that we were doing everything badly, and all the time, won out. If mindfulness, the individualistic wellness model that triumphed in the years preceding the pandemic, is defined in part as the capacity to fully inhabit the moment, to focus on the here and now, my experience since I became a mother, particularly in moments of stress, is its complete opposite.

I don't suspect I'd get rich writing a manual on mindlessness, an invented discipline in which I consider myself an expert: how to constantly feel that you're in the wrong place, with your mind somewhere else entirely. There and then, rather than here and now.

You will have achieved the pinnacle of mindlessness, I would write in my manual of self-sabotage for beginners, when you tense up after ten hours working at the computer, feeling you should be playing with modelling clay with your children, or at least making them dinner. It's also peak mindlessness to read your child a story while periodically checking the time on your phone, calculating whether half an hour of *The Gruffalo's Child* is enough, as if someone is keeping track of all this, as if they'll rule, in the end, in favour of the plaintiff.

In 1937, Muriel Camberg married a man thirteen years her senior, whom she barely knew. His name was Sidney Oswald Spark, and it wasn't long before Muriel was referring to him by his initials, as if making a private joke: SOS. Help, I married a stranger.

SOS, who went by Solly, was a secular Jew and had been born in Lithuania, as was Barry, the writer's father. At thirty-two years old, he was working as a maths teacher in Edinburgh.

They met at a dance put on by the Over-Seas League, an event of the type Muriel often attended with her only brother, Philipp. Despite their age difference and Solly's somewhat taciturn character, he and Muriel connected. They both liked to talk about books, and together they listened to the radio broadcast during which Edward VIII abdicated the throne for the promise of a life at once more mundane and more exotic with Wallis Simpson. Sidney also suggested to Muriel – and this is crucial – the possibility of a vague future beyond provincial Edinburgh. The teacher had been planning to travel to Africa, find work there and visit the colonies. In Rhodesia, he promised Muriel, hiring help was much less expensive. They could afford to have servants, and Muriel wouldn't have to act as a housewife.

That was a tempting offer for a woman who already saw quite clearly that she had outgrown the life her birthplace and her social class assigned her. When she was a young girl, her favourite teacher, Miss Kay, had dazzled her with tales of her travels to Egypt, Rome, and Switzerland. The charismatic Miss Kay took Muriel and her friend Frances to see the latest Pavlova performance at the Edinburgh Empire Theatre, followed by tea at the elegant McVitie's tearoom. Spark commandeered an expression (and plenty of other things) from her teacher and gave it to her most famous character, Miss Brodie, the at once innocent and manipulative protagonist who gives full meaning to *The Prime of Miss Jean Brodie*. For Jean Brodie, as for Miss Kay, anything good was 'the crème de la crème'. It's impossible to read those words without hearing them in the accent Maggie Smith puts on in the film adaptation. Smith pronounces them with a fabulous *r*, much more Scottish than French. 'My students are the crrrème de la crrrème,' she says. That moment encapsulates all the pretension of Jean Brodie, a woman as ridiculous as she is real.

After a year of sexless courtship, Muriel and Solly got married, shared a wedding night the bride later described as 'a botch-up', and went to live in Rhodesia. The first place where the precarious couple settled was Fort Victoria (Masvingo), a small and dusty city. The country, one of those British colonial inventions, was named after the politician and magnate Cecil Rhodes and had only existed as such for fifty-something years. Its population was made up of one and a half million Africans and about fifty-five thousand European colonists who behaved as if the systems they'd put in place, based on the most elementary racism, were going to last forever.

A few weeks after arriving in Fort Victoria, SOS was already having problems with the authorities at the school where he had been contracted. He began to show signs of mental unwellness, and conflict followed wherever he went.

Muriel once asked him why he had never told her about his tenuous mental health. He replied that, had she known, she never would have married him. The logic was indisputable.

Shortly after that confession, Muriel became pregnant. He proposed an abortion, she refused; though she wasn't longing to become a parent either, much less to perpetuate that marriage, which she already saw as an error, by bringing a child into the world.

Robin Spark was born on 9 July 1938, in the Bulawayo hospital, following a day and a half of extremely difficult labour. Muriel describes it in her memoir, *Curriculum Vitae*, published in 1992: 'I was at the end of my strength and didn't expect that either I or my baby would survive, and, indeed, it was a miracle that we both emerged strong and healthy. I had bitten down one of my nails. My husband brought me a manicure set and a bunch of flowers. He began to show signs of the severe nervous disorder from which he had suffered and was to suffer all his life. He had fits of violence, and continued to quarrel with everybody.'

An author as sharp and precise as Muriel Spark doesn't construct a paragraph that way by accident. Her only son is born. She breaks a nail. Her husband begins to become a nightmare. Everything condensed into three hundred words, less than they used to explain the plot of a movie back when newspapers still had movie listings, less than you'd write in a work email to postpone a meeting and propose a new date. That very compact synthesis is entirely intentional.

In *Muriel Spark: The Biography*, biographer Martin Stannard maintains that for his mother, Robin would always be a by-product of her unhappy marriage; that she was never able to separate the child from his father, and that when she looked at her son, the first thing she saw was the face of that mediocre and violent man whom she'd outgrown in two afternoons.

The chronology of the following years in Muriel's life is hazy, and she herself contributed to the confusion in varying accounts of her years in Africa. Immediately after the birth of her son, Muriel stopped producing milk and fell into postpartum depression, though no one at that time would have diagnosed it as such. Muriel and Solly never slept together again, or so she wrote. He reached the point of assaulting her, and she had to hide the revolver her husband kept in their home, like almost all white men in Africa, for fear that he would shoot her. It wasn't an entirely paranoid thought: in the very hotel where Muriel was then living with Solly and the baby, she had re-encountered an old school friend from Edinburgh. Redheaded like her, Nita McEwan was known as Muriel's doppelgänger. One night, the writer heard an unusual noise. In the morning, she learned that Nita's husband had shot and killed her in cold blood then killed himself. She wrote about it in the story

'Bang-Bang, You're Dead', in which the protagonist, Sybil, survives because her husband accidentally murders the neighbour, whom she closely resembles.

At last, Muriel managed to separate from SOS, at least practically speaking. He had work at a military detachment in Gwelo, and she combined several jobs as a typographer and secretary at various companies in Bulawayo. She shared a flat with May Haygate, a friend whose husband was in the army and who also had a small child. In December 1939, the writer tried to get a divorce. They didn't make it easy. According to colonial law, neither the mental instability nor the cruelty she accused her husband of were sufficient basis for her to be granted a divorce, which she would not achieve legally until four years later. The only grounds considered valid were adultery or desertion. 'He was not going to desert me, so I deserted him,' she wrote years later. 'Life in the colony was eating my heart away.'

Muriel needed to get out of Africa, but with the war ongoing, travel with children was strictly forbidden. So she left Robin, who was then four years old, at a convent in Gwelo, and moved to the city of Salisbury, in Southern Rhodesia, to wait for the divorce to be finalised.

'I decided for my sanity's sake to go ahead by myself,' she explains in *Curriculum Vitae*, where she describes an expeditious separation from her son, as a practical arrangement, framing it in a context of international turmoil: 'I had met some very good Catholic nuns at the Dominican convent school in Gwelo. Quite a few young children separated from their parents by the war were at boarding school there. I was satisfied that Robin would be safe in that convent school. Even my husband in the mental home, asserting on paper his legal "rights", liked the nuns of Gwelo. Robin was able to play with the children of my friends there. A friendly professional childminder and her family had

Robin home almost every day, and supported me greatly with constant letters.' It's clear that Spark has little desire to discuss the matter, but also that she feels some need to justify her decision before the reader. The nuns were good. The boy was happy. I left because I had to leave.

In her memoir, Spark skips over the two years mother and son spent on different continents: 'My plan,' she continues, 'was to prepare for Robin to go and live with my parents, who were pining to have him as soon as the war was over and the transport ban lifted. This worked remarkably well. I arrived in England in March 1944. My little son joined me in September of the following year and was greeted with great joy by both my parents.'

As a contemporary reader, gorging on memoirs and auto-fictional writing, I'm struck by how reserved and modest Spark's memoir is about everything related to her son, as if she were holding any hint of sentimentality at such a distance that she ended up writing something almost clinical. This is not uncommon; it happens in the memoirs of other sublime writers, like Edith Wharton, who seems incapable of applying the charm that abounds in her fiction to her own life. Although in Spark's case, there's something else at play. At the time of writing, it was already clear that her relationship with Robin was a disaster, and maybe she didn't feel up to describing that irretrievable bond.

The reader can tell Spark is eager to settle the issue and make clear that there was no problem at all, that the child was born and was never a burden, a weight, a question mark. Poet Elaine Feinstein, who wrote the foreword for the reissue, goes so far as to say that Spark 'does not seem to have been unduly troubled' by the abandonment. Feinstein, another judge.

Spark devotes many more pages of her memoir to, for example, her dramas at the *Poetry Review*, where during her term as editor, she turned all of England's poetry old guard against her, or the challenges of publishing her books, the arrangements she made with her publishers, and the circumstances under which she wrote some of her novels. But she doesn't devote a single line to her pregnancy. On the other hand, why should she have to? Writing about what happened inside of her uterus would have been the equivalent of a male writer of the 1950s and 60s (the most fruitful years of her career) describing his problems during a colonic. Something dirty, perhaps vulgar.

Even at the beginning of the nineties, when this memoir was published, it was still unusual for women writers to explore that side of their experience. Not so now, when the opposite is true and there's a much higher degree of intimacy expected in women's writing than men's. Women are expected to spill their bodily fluids across the page and drench their novels, essays, and interviews in confessions, the stickier the better. Otherwise, the reader, and certainly the interviewer, feels as if something is being withheld. As if they're only getting scraps. I know because I often am that interviewer, asking for blood, or at least sweat.

It's a recurring theme now in the literary conversation among women; how women writers, and especially debut women writers, are expected to hand over their lives in bits and pieces so the reader can make a table centrepiece with them. 'Writing and publishing a novel are antithetical experiences,' author Olivia Sudjic writes in her book *Exposure*. 'The material, no matter the subject, is, by nature, personal. [The writer] protects it, and herself, from the "real" world, sometimes for years, guarding against seepage, contamination, exposure. Then, when it comes to publication (and promotion!) of the work, this laying bare, especially for a debut novelist, is a Saturn Return that may be sudden and painful, even for someone fairly extroverted in their non-writing life. On top of the multiple fictional mindsets they must harbour within their own, novelists now need split personalities.'

But Spark wasn't in that business, not in 1992, and if her relationship with her only son was traumatic, she felt no need to incorporate that subsection of her life into her literary legacy. She hadn't written twenty-two novels so she could be talked about as a mother and not as an author, she must have thought, relying on basic jurisprudence. No male writer was being judged as a father. That only came much later, when, for example, Pablo Neruda and Arthur Miller were denounced for ridding themselves of their sick children. When people like Susan Cheever wrote memoirs about their fathers, fathers who never felt that their problems with elusive literary glory had anything to do with the perfectly normal fact of having children.

After the time they spent apart, Robin and Muriel never again had a smooth relationship. The family harboured the vague idea that the boy would reunite with his mother and go and live with her in London once she had earned enough money, but that never became a reality, and over the years, a resentment and kind of mutual estrangement grew between them.

Muriel's conversion to Catholicism amplified their differences, further dividing the two parts of the family. On one hand were the Jewish Cambergs in Edinburgh, and on the other, Catholic Spark, in London and beyond. Muriel's decision to retain the surname from her failed marriage to SOS is common enough in the Anglo-Saxon world, but there has been speculation around the interest she may have had in going through life with a name that sounded much more Anglo and less Semitic than the one she was given at birth. In 1952, when Muriel had already become a successful writer, Robin wanted to celebrate his bar mitzvah. His mother sent him the fifty pounds she had won from the *Observer* for a literary prize so the grandparents could host a luncheon afterwards, but knowing that her ex-husband would be there – he too had returned from Rhodesia, and without getting rich, as many others there had – she declined to attend. And that ratcheted up the tension between mother and son.

There were other similar episodes, which only made clear how little Muriel and Robin understood each other. Every year, she forced herself to holiday with the family in the village of Morecambe, embarking on stale excursions around the Lake District. She kept arranging these visits in hopes of achieving what, in the realm of affluent motherhood, is now known as *bonding*, creating links, spending quality time. Muriel came away from those painful trips with nothing but frozen feet – why go to the damn Lakes if what she preferred was Italy, or New York – and a growing sense that she had nothing in common with her own son.

One of her lovers during that time, the dilettante Howard Sergeant, came to visit her in Edinburgh when Robin was seven years old. Although she was a divorced adult woman who paid many of the expenses of her parents' household, Muriel couldn't simply turn up with a boyfriend, so Sergeant stayed at the Caledonian Hotel, one of the most luxurious in the city. He wrote about the dynamic he witnessed during the trip and which she later recorded in her memoir:

It was very interesting to see Muriel in her home circle. It was obvious that she felt out of place and that the family irritated her. Even Robin got on her nerves and she showed little patience – this, I gather, is the result of a conflict in her mind. Mrs. Camberg has, quite naturally, taken Muriel's place as a mother to Robin, who looks upon Muriel as someone who visits him occasionally and gives him presents. Robin is frequently rude and unpleasant to Muriel, but that again is a psychological effect. . . . [She] prefers being financially responsible but having no other ties. At the same time there is a resentment both to Robin and Mrs. Camberg. There seems little maternal feeling in Muriel – but she may have been suppressing.

The dynamic Sergeant describes, of the grandmother acting as mother and seeing the birth mother as an intruder who interferes with the child's routines, is familiar to many women who have had to leave their children in the care of their parents in order to work in another country. As time goes by, they watch that space between the grandmother and the child, the gap that would correspond to them, become increasingly uncomfortable and narrow. Nobody knows what to do with them when they return. They're a nuisance.

While all this was going on, Muriel lived in London, and later New York, where she worked for spells in an office on the premises of *The New Yorker*. Those years make for the brightest and most exciting part of her memoir. From that small office, she could see a red neon sign in Rockefeller Center: *Time / Life*, it read, referring to the magazines. 'When it says Time, I write. When it says Life, I want to go out,' she told a friend, as described in her biography by Martin Stannard. In fact she had time to do both, to live and to write. In New York she stayed in a flat at the Beaux Arts Hotel, and in a month, she finished one of her best novels, *The Girls of Slender Means*.

Meanwhile, in Edinburgh, her recently widowed mother, Cissy, was looking after Robin. Could Spark have written with such lightness and concentration if she'd had to prepare two or three meals a day for a small child? Who knows, but it isn't likely. She possessed a rare combination of talent, determination, diligence, and hunger for glory. She was able to quickly seize the writer's ego one needs to get ahead in the publishing world. But even the writer-mother with the best-equipped ego has to stop from time to time to gather Legos from the floor. Even the writer-mother most confident in her calling will find that the sentences simply don't flow as they should after a sleepless night helping her child through a stomach virus. It's easy to conclude that she would have written, but perhaps not so much.

During the pandemic lockdown, I continued to deliver all the articles they asked for, obliged to work more to earn less. I also kept my children fed, clothed (mostly), and emotionally healthy to a reasonable degree.

What I didn't do was finish the book I was supposed to write in those months. I thought what we were living through rendered it meaningless. Or that's what I told myself. In those days, it seemed that nothing we'd known pre-Covid would be valid afterwards, although later, as restaurants reopened for outdoor dining and there was more than just pandemic talk on the radio, the same debates we had put on hold steadily resumed.

Surely I also abandoned the project because I lacked the courage to put it before everything else. I could doubtless have awoken at five in the morning and taken better advantage of the quiet hours, as so many women writers do, accustomed to working in silence and darkness while their children are asleep. I could have done fewer puzzles, made fewer cupcakes, done a little less self-sabotage by way of overcommitting to other projects, insisted instead on redirecting my dwindling energy to that sad manuscript so it would make sense after Covid, urged myself on a little harder, cultivating my voice and a little ego to match.

Nor was I practising motherhood with any degree of excellence. I continued to be a distracted mother, prone to outbursts, inconsistent, impatient. 'At least the kids are all right,' I wrote to the other mothers again, when they were the ones feeling low and in need of a throwaway phrase. At that point in the pandemic, words like those weren't just worn out, they were now a crusted rag we passed back and forth without any conviction. There was a part two that we never wrote, after 'the kids are all right'. The part that said, 'Are we really going to settle for that?'

Muriel did exactly what so many men have done: covered the cost of her child from a distance. When Robin turned nineteen, she took him to Nice on holiday, thinking that a more relaxed environment might loosen up their relationship, but those days proved disastrous as well. The mother thought things would improve now that they could talk like two adults, if he would only shake off the provincialism of Edinburgh and become a little more worldly, more crème de la crème. She invited him to spend time in London, where she proudly paraded him around at parties. But the friendship she had envisioned between two people with barely twenty years between them never came to be.

In their final disagreement, the issue of faith reared its head again. Both in her interviews and in her memoir, the author always conveyed that in her childhood home, Judaism was practised in as lax a manner as possible; that the Cambergs were 'cultural Jews' or 'Gentile Jews' – she even wrote an autobiographical story entitled 'The Gentile Jewesses' – with little or no attachment to religion. Robin, on the other hand, who had become quite attached to Judaism, had a very different understanding of the family history and wanted to cast upon his mother the idea of a shame-based conversion to Catholicism, inspired by a kind of self-loathing. Either that or he simply found the most convenient path to hurting his mother.

In 1998, Robin Spark summoned the press to tell them he had obtained his grandparents' marriage certificate, their ketubah, which said their wedding had taken place in the East London synagogue. The existence of the document implied that both Muriel's father and mother had been Jewish by origin, not just her father, as Muriel had maintained. The London press covered this seemingly minor story at length because it meant the famous writer might have been lying and because it had elements – 'Catholic conversion' and 'feud between mother and son' – that drew enough curiosity to serve as the subjects of five articles.

Having run out of patience, the author responded to the press: '[My son] has got in on the act because he wants publicity . . . He can't sell his lousy paintings and I have had a lot of success . . . he's never done anything for me, except for being one big bore.' And after that episode, she would refuse to ever see him again or have any contact with him. Whenever she had to go back to Edinburgh for work, usually to be feted as the most renowned living Scottish author, she stayed with Penelope Jardine in a hotel.

It would be too simplistic to conclude that Muriel Spark traded a son for a literary career. The scope of what she achieved as an author is enormous in itself, but even more staggering when one considers that she was a working-class woman, peripheral by birth, lacking a strong tie to her country of origin – her relationship with Scotland was almost as complicated as the one she had with Robin – and had no university training, nor patrons besides the ones she earned with her own talents. It's easy to assume that in addition to a full life and a successful career, she would have liked to have had, on top of or in the midst of all that, a good relationship with her only child. But that didn't happen. Even in the most expansive lives, and hers was one of them, not everything fits.

Good Bad Mothers and Bad Bad Mothers

There's a journalistic genre I've consumed avidly, sometimes a little shamefully, since I was twenty years old: first-person essays about life experiences, almost always written by women. Their popularity reached its peak at the beginning of the 2000s, in pre-Twitter times, when Facebook was just a place where you announced parties and there was still something resembling the artisanal internet, with digital media that wasn't necessarily attached to a massive corporation.

Those years saw the forging of a first-person industry whose influence is undeniable in much of today's most highly regarded literature, in the essays and memoirs in which 'the best thing they have to offer is the worst thing that ever happened to them', as Jia Tolentino is quoted as saying in Laura Bennett's article 'The First-Person Industrial Complex'. Tolentino herself was for a while in charge of publishing precisely these kinds of texts for the feminist website *Jezebel*, before she moved on to write for *The New Yorker*. First-person essays took a special hold in digital media, like Jezebel or xoJane, which brought the genre to a fever pitch with articles like: 'It Happened to Me: My Friend Joined ISIS' or 'My Gynaecologist Found a Ball of Cat Hair in My Vagina'.

That was also the period when I began to think I would end

up becoming a mother; not right away, but later, when I had achieved a superior state of being: the Mother Version. Back then I had a vague notion that as the years passed I would keep updating, like the iOS on my phone, and at some point I'd reach that optimal state, the one that was finally compatible with motherhood. I now know that's not how it goes. You just carry on, defects and all, even accumulating new ones, and if you do decide to have children at some point, you concentrate on hiding them from your descendants.

Many of the essays I was reading then were about motherhood, and I suspect that I was using them as a manual and also, in some cases, a form of homeopathy, or a votive offering. Maybe by reading this, by taking a small dose of this particular maternal horror, I'll inoculate myself, and it won't happen to me. That's how magical thinking works.

Digital media served me them by the dozen, one after another: How I realised my baby was on the autism spectrum. How my marriage fell apart after my son was born. How I lost all my friends who didn't have children. How my vagina became unrecognisable. I devoured them, part horrified, part fascinated, at every brow height within which cultural products used to be classified: lowbrow, middlebrow, even vaguely highbrow.

When I became pregnant and realised I did indeed want to have the child, all those texts formed a slick magma in my head, which served to generate new and specific fears. Fear of never reading again – that came from tweets and dubiously tongue-in-cheek comments from mums who said they hadn't finished a novel in three years – fear of turning into a person no one wanted to talk to, fear of having nothing to say; fear, in conclusion, of being nothing more than a damn mother.

During the first two weeks of that pregnancy, before I had told people about it, I functioned more or less normally during the day, and at night, I sat down on the sofa and cried. It wasn't dramatic, but it was methodical and consistent. Those were the years of *Españoles en el mundo*. There was something on every channel along those lines – a programme where the entire focus was interviewing Spanish people living sometimes exciting, sometimes nonsensical lives abroad. You turned on the TV and there was a guy from Murcia living in Azerbaijan, then one from Castelldefels, so happy in New Zealand. I watched them and felt angst. What about me? When was I going to live in New York or Berlin, as my entire generation had planned to do and, in some cases, done? The least original aspiration in the world. An overworked wish. What twists will I incorporate into my life if it's entirely defined by obligation and routine, if all that awaits me now is being a mother, anchored to this place, fixed to this circumstance?

On those ten or fifteen nights, I sat on the white sofa (years later, it had to be reupholstered in blue, the white didn't work with kids) next to my partner, who didn't cry – on the contrary, he went to great lengths not to annoy me with his pure, indisputable joy – and said goodbye to all the lives I'd never have one by one, all the hypotheses that had been replaced, or so I believed then, by a single certainty, the mother of all certainties.

I didn't realise that there is little predictability in pregnancies. That particular one ended in the two worst ways a pregnancy can end, when taken together: late, and badly. And after that loss, all that was left was an animal need to have a child. From that moment on, and until I became pregnant again not long after, all the other life hypotheses seemed disposable. Almost everyone who has spent a length of time obsessed with conceiving knows how promptly it colonises your imagination, leaving no space for anything else.

Meanwhile, I kept reading articles written in the first person.

How I became an alcoholic when I became a mother. How we battled the worst diagnosis we could possibly have received. How I learned to love my mum hips.

The only one I never read, because I never came across it on my usual websites and no algorithm sent it my way, is 'Why I Left My Children' or 'How I Made the Decision to Abandon My Children'. It's easier to find a first-person essay about a sexual relationship between a daughter and her biological father (there are many, and a few documentaries, too) than to read about a woman who voluntarily gives up care of her children.

The first one Google offered up when I searched for 'why I left my kids' was a very brief article published in 2021, in the magazine *Today's Parent*: 'I Left My Kids and Husband to Find Myself'.

The author begins by outlining her case, searching for exoneration from the reader with the right dose of self-flagellation, as generally happens in these texts. She writes in the article that she married a controlling man, had to leave her job to care for her children, and also put her dream of writing fiction on hold – the husband wouldn't allow her to apply for a master's in creative writing. The husband, she says, was adamant they do things as a family, and she couldn't go on holiday with friends, or go out to eat, or to movies. So she decided to get a divorce, and the judge only granted her 40 per cent of the time with the kids, who were then eleven and eight years old.

When it comes to the standard version of these kinds of articles, the formula indicates that they must end with a kind of self-validation, with evidence that the undersigned did, in the end, what was right. This text is no exception. The author admits that the separation was painful for the kids but that ultimately she was able to strengthen her relationship with them while also feeling present with herself again.

Medium, the platform for what it self-describes as 'social journalism', created to help a wide range of personal texts find their niche, doesn't offer much in the way of literature about mothers who leave either, despite the fact that millions of articles have been published there. Everything from a generic 'I may not like my husband anymore, but I still love him' to the very specific 'What my autistic son's fear of biking taught me about guilt'.

In this vast web of confessional writing, there is only one article, written by Michon Neal in 2016, that explains why a mother decided to live kilometres away from her three-year-old son. The cause is a very heavy one: she needed to get away from the small city where the man who raped her and the people he associates with still live. Neal confesses that she has only seen her son twice in the last year, that she thinks of him every time she crosses paths with a child, and that sometimes it's painful for him as well. 'I don't want him growing up thinking that mothers don't have their own lives outside of their children, that any parent doesn't have a life outside of their child. I don't want him to sacrifice his dreams, his sanity, health, or his sense of worth for anyone. I don't want him to go crazy trying to do "the right thing",' she concludes in the obligatory self-affirming paragraph. 'Am I a bad mother for spending a year away from him?' she asks. 'It's not easy but I believe he's worth it, and so am I.'

A similarly titled first-person essay – 'Why I Left My Children' – was published in the magazine *Salon* in 2011. In the second paragraph, it becomes clear that the author, Rahna Reiko Rizzuto, didn't abandon her children, exactly, but rather accepted a grant that entailed her moving to Japan from the United States for six months, during which time her children would remain with their father. If a heterosexual male writer or journalist wanted to publish something like that, he would immediately be met with a certain reluctance from his editor.

'So, let's hear it. You say they're giving you a grant.'

'Yes, that's right.'

'And you're going to be away for a while, doing research.'

'Exactly.'

'And your kids will be with their mother.'

'Right.'

'I'm sorry, but I'm not following. Where's the story?'

When I was at university, they taught us that the strange things, the surprising ones, will always be news. Journalism has changed a lot since then, but also not that much.

Rahna Reiko Rizzuto accepted her grant. She went to Japan alone, and barely two months later, her marriage fell apart. The couple separated and the writer gave up custody of the children. She moved into a house on the same street as her ex-husband and focused on acting as a parent during 'blocks of time' when she could devote herself, she says, to being 'that 1950s mother we idealize who was waiting in an apron with fresh cookies'.

After the divorce, when she realised she had never actually wanted to be a mother, she could practise motherhood as separated fathers traditionally have, before shared custody became fashionable, scooping up her kids for some holidays and half the summer vacation.

In 2010 Rahna Reiko Rizzuto wrote a book called *Hiroshima in the Morning*, with a premise that was risky, to say the least: she mixed the work she had actually gone to Japan to do – interviewing survivors of the atomic bomb – with her own experiences, her separation from her children, and her ambiguous feelings about what it meant to be a mother. The book was praised and named a finalist for the National Book Critics Circle Award in the US. But at the same time, it earned the author a wave of abuse and insults, on- and offline. Her neighbours crossed the street to avoid greeting her. On the internet, she received hundreds of hostile comments and the kinds of death threats and sexual aggression that are shared currency between women in digital discourse. They called her 'garbage' and 'worse than Hitler'. Complete strangers would stop her and ask: 'How could you have abandoned your children?' which she found shocking, since many times they said this in front of her children, who were there with her, in the beverage aisle at the supermarket.

Reiko Rizzuto wrote:

> The hostility and abuse that is directed at the 'mother who leaves' clearly does not depend on her actual leaving. We want our mothers to be long-suffering, to put their children's needs first and their own well-being last if there is time left. We need her to get dinner on the table and the laundry done and the kids to school and the homework finished and the house clean and the cookies for the bake sale made and the school clothes purchased. Our society is hurting, schools are bankrupt, family finances are squeezed, drugs and guns and sex in the media and international terror are all bombarding our children and the person we designate to help kids negotiate all of this is their mother. It's a big job, too big for one person. Especially when she also has to work, and when she also has a life of her own to care for. But to say that, to act on it, is too much of a threat.

After she published the book, the media briefly upheld her as a kind of spokesperson for mothers who have elected not to live with their children. Promotion of her work, as might be expected, cast aside all reference to Hiroshima in favour of the most titillating aspect: her family story. The author accepted the deal: they would talk about her in exchange for her running the risk of being called the two words no one wants to hear: 'bad mother'.

Bad bad mother, you understand, not *good* bad mother. Being a good bad mother is acknowledged, even accepted, and is the daily bread of many Instagram mums and previously some blog moms. The good bad mother discourse shapes the dialect used in WhatsApp parent groups; a lightly comic, modestly self-lacerating language that seems easy enough to pick up, but deceptively so, because the rules governing it are very specific. There's a subtle line between what can and cannot be said. Learning to recognise that barrier is crucial, because those who get it wrong will cause a communicative rift, a glitch in the system.

In Spain, there's even a very powerful group called the Bad Mums Club, which was born on Facebook and has ended up serving as a kind of lobby, in the most benign sense of the term. They post very useful studies on motherhood and work-life balance, and they get a lot of media and political attention. Shortly after becoming prime minister, Pedro Sánchez attended an action organised by the Bad Mums Club, in shorts and a fluorescent t-shirt, and took the opportunity to make political promises about universal preschool education and the types of legislative initiatives that are believed to be of consequence only for women.

Beyond that concrete collective, the idea of the bad mother that triumphs on the internet is the mother who buys the costume for the school play on Amazon instead of sewing it herself; or the one who brings a cake from a supermarket for the birthday party instead of a homemade version baked with spelt flour; or who, one rainy Saturday, lets the kids stay in their pyjamas for eight hours of screen time in a row and then says so in a tweet that gets plenty of likes. The good bad mum is the one who gently and mischievously subverts the recognisable expectations of normative middle-class parenting, but without ever overdoing it. Availing oneself of the good-bad-mum stereotype, prevalent in recent years in TV series of the subgenre mum-in-distress (there are rows and rows on the Netflix menu devoted to this subject), means very carefully measuring how far one can take the transgression. Never under any circumstance will the umbrella of the good bad mum shelter a woman who chooses voluntarily not to live with her children.

In fact, there are many additional ways to garner hatred on the internet for being a bad mum. My only experiences in this area are quite minor, but at the time they caused me anxiety, like any exchange of digital hostilities.

Though I read many articles on the subject, I don't often write about being a mother, nor about my own children. I'm a passive audience when it comes to the topic of motherhood. Early on after having children, I made this choice out of a mixture of strategy and self-abnegation. I never mentioned my child as grounds not to accept a job, preferring to allege too much work, sickness, or anything else rather than remind my employers that in addition to being a versatile and always alert writer, I was also a mother. I resisted being categorised as the girl who writes about 'mum things', someone who is no longer in the know, who misses everything that matters because she's too busy posting about baby-led weaning in mum chats. It's striking – or depressing, depending on your point of view – the degree to which anything that has to do with motherhood is devalued in a profession as feminised as journalism. I understood this instinctively when I arrived as a twenty-something to my first editorial office at a large media outlet. All the men had children, none of the women had them. In twenty years, not a single woman editor or photographer (that was easy – there were no women photographers) had found herself in the predicament of requesting parental leave at that newspaper.

The tendency to pretend is nipped in the bud when the second child arrives, according to my observations. At that point, deception is no longer a possibility. With two children there's no helping it: the world sees you as a mother. No one can get you out of there now, and any attempt to do so will lead to frustration. It makes sense. If you've had two children, there's no chance that it was an accident. You got yourself into this, and on top of that, you're a reoffender.

The few times I've broken my own rule of not writing about issues related to motherhood, I've been burned. And it's no coincidence. Publishing articles on raising children almost guarantees controversy. You can write about the Catalan independence movement, discuss whether there should be a *cordon sanitaire* around Vox's far-right views, analyse whether a slice of Spain is empty or has been emptied, or challenge surrogate pregnancy. You can adopt an immovable stance on any single issue. The gender self-identification law. Labour reform. Rent control. The 'parental veto' on education. Nothing will invite as much visceral debate as the things we do with our children in the privacy of our homes.

On one occasion, I was accused of encouraging foetal alcohol syndrome by writing about the work of Emily Oster, a researcher focusing on health economics and statistical methods who has written three books about pregnancy and child-rearing. Oster represents an optimised, outcome-oriented form of mothering that could be seen to have a sinister side, and the approach that made her famous involves questioning the way some studies have been used to impose measures that infantilise women instead of to illuminate shadowy areas. One section of her first book, *Expecting Better*, centres on the well-known recommendation not to drink alcohol during pregnancy. Oster concludes there is no clear evidence that consuming a very moderate amount of alcohol harms the foetus, while a high level of consumption is shown to.

I made several mistakes when I wrote that article. To begin with, by pitching it in the first place, since I never should have taken on that subject in a section where the pieces are very short and there's little space for nuance. Then, by not checking the title and subtitle they assigned me – it's common practice in the media for the journalist not to write those herself. The thing is, I reviewed that text dozens of times before sending it in, softening the verbs, adjusting the wording, and doing everything I could to avoid a backlash that I could see coming, but I paid so much attention to one part of the article, which discussed lactation – a subject that, whenever and wherever it comes up, is destined to generate a cataclysm of opinions that can only escalate in intensity, in which no one, ever, under any circumstance, will modify the opinion they brought from home by one iota, and in which every participant will emerge scathed – that I didn't sufficiently apply myself to disarming the other subject, consumption of alcohol during pregnancy.

The article caused a brief but resounding controversy. Several readers called me irresponsible and homicidal, and as often happens, they hurled their quotation marks down upon me: 'journalist', you call yourself a 'journalist'. There are people who believe nothing hurts as much as quotation marks.

I got through it by leaving Twitter for a few days and sending my clarification – that there were no inaccuracies in the text and that all Oster's data was backed by evidence – to the Reader's Ombudsman at the newspaper, who had requested it due to the wave of escalating complaints, some of them from medical associations.

On the other side of that episode, I swore I would never again try to write about anything related to pregnancy, mother-hood, or child-rearing, because whatever the fee for the article, it will never cover the sleepless nights you spend listening to your phone vibrate in the dark, certain each intermittent sound signals a new insult. A journalist friend who, like all my woman journalist friends, has several times endured the digital mob, described the strange dissociative sensation you experience as you more or less carry on with your life while they attack you on Twitter: 'The kid had the tablet, he was watching *Peppa Pig*, and every two seconds another notification, someone else calling me a fucking bitch. Good thing the kid can't read.'

Despite my best efforts, I would occasionally relapse, with similar results. I very deliberately pitched an interview with Sophie Lewis, a Marxist sociologist who has developed a theory on abolishing the family. The article was published in the days before Christmas Eve. 'I hope you rot alone with your cats,' they said on Twitter, just as I was finishing wrapping up gifts, preparing for the most gruellingly normative time of year with my very heteronormative two-parent family.

Around that same time, I had an idea for an article I thought would be light, funny, frivolous, despite being related to mother-hood, about the experience of watching the movie *Soul* with my children. Although I liked the film, I said I preferred the part in which the protagonist, Joe, is on Earth, with his mother, his students, and his work frustrations, to the complicated metaphysical architecture of the rest of the screenplay, and that in general Pixar movies are becoming harder and harder for children to understand. For expressing such a radical opinion, I was a trending topic the day after Christmas when Twitter was looking to debate something other than the pandemic, which was at that point in its extremely dangerous second wave. Several hundred users expressed pity for my children, who I'd thought – good plan – to mention in the article, for having a mother so obtuse she was ignorant of the fact that children have feelings. Thankfully, there was a minor quake in the Spanish political landscape that made them forget all about me.

When you're suffering viral attention – which I don't recommend to anyone who's not afflicted with narcissistic personality disorder – your friends and acquaintances send condolences and hugs, and the more they try to console you, the more distressed you'll become. Something terrible must be happening out there, you think, while you take refuge behind your privacy settings and resist the temptation to look at your mentions, these days at fifty-plus, which is how the social network communicates you're in trouble. After a certain number, Twitter doesn't even bother to properly count the number of people who want to insult you, they just say that it's above fifty, that they're waiting with clubs outside your house.

In any case, my pretty laughable controversies – there are much worse digital ordeals, suffered disproportionately by women, people of colour, and members of the LGBTQ+ community – offered me a minuscule sample of what it must be like to receive, on social media, the worst epithet of all: bad mother.

In 2005, or in other words, four or five internets ago, the writer and screenwriter Ayelet Waldman wrote an article for the famous 'Modern Love' section of the *New York Times*, with a premise that, right from the outset, invited trouble: that if, in a kind of hypothetical Sophie's choice, she had to choose between losing her husband (the writer Michael Chabon), or losing one of her four children, she would choose the latter. 'If a good mother is one who loves her child more than anyone else in the world, I am not a good mother. I am in fact a bad mother. I love my husband more than I love my children.'

Although at that point Twitter didn't exist, lucky for Waldman, indignant readers found a way to convey to the author how monstrous, inhuman, satanic they considered her for making such a claim. She defended herself on *The Oprah Winfrey Show*. And later she capitalised on the uproar with a book entitled *Bad Mother*.

Since then, many other women have competed for the title of 'bad mother' on the internet. Due to excess or deficiency, smothering their children or the complete opposite. The bad mother of 2011 was Amy Chua, self-branded later as a 'tiger mother'. Chua wrote an article in the *Wall Street Journal* defending her style of parenting, one of Chinese parents who demand perfection from their children and don't waste time on silly things like emotional well-being, or so the stereotype goes. The text – I imagine the digital editor at the *WSJ* posting it on social media like someone throwing a hand grenade then fleeing the explosion, flames behind him – was bannered with a photograph of Chua and her two daughters, one playing violin, the other at a piano, and opened with a list of things the girls were not allowed to do: have a playdate, attend a sleepover, be in a school play, complain about not being in a school play. Those kinds of things would have diverted them from academic excellence and therefore were prohibited in the Chua household. That woman's commitment to her method, and to becoming famous, went quite far. In the book she wrote to capitalise on the article's success, she broadened the notion of the 'tiger mother' and recounted how, for example, she called her daughter 'garbage' for disrespecting her; how she threatened to burn their stuffed animals; that once, one girl fainted from exhaustion after practising piano for so many hours, and her teeth left marks on the keys.

Following that episode, Chua and her husband, Jed Rubenfeld, both of them Yale Law power brokers, were established as conservative trolls in the American media landscape. They co-wrote a book that was immediately branded as racist about why certain cultural groups triumph when they immigrate and others don't. Later on, he was publicly accused of a pattern of sexual misconduct and was suspended after an inquiry, while she was accused of grooming, selecting only female students who looked 'like models' to be clerks for a conservative Supreme Court judge (even though she has always denied these claims). Their opponents revelled in their double fall from grace, the sweet taste of schadenfreude. Finally, that terrible mother got what she deserved. Their delight only could have been greater if the two girls had turned out badly. At present, it's only known that both have studied at Yale Law School.

If Chua was the bad mother of the right, Lenore Skenazy was the progressive version. She caused outrage in 2009 by announcing that she had let her nine-year-old son take the subway in New York City alone and defending 'free-range parenting'. They dubbed her 'the worst mother in America', and she, too, monetised it with a book, a blog, and media appearances. Of course, many nine-year-old children in New York take the train alone and make themselves dinner. They're almost always children of single, working mothers, and no one asks them to write books or articles on the subject.

There's another way to become a dubious mother in the eyes of the public, and it has less to do with one's parenting style and more to do with one's attitude towards motherhood. The German photographer Sarah Fischer prompted a fevered discussion in her country when, in 2016, she published a book entitled *Die Mutterglück-Lüge* (*The Mother-Bliss Lie*), in which she declared that she loved her two-year-old daughter very much but at the same time regretted having had her. Fischer explains in the book that she went from travelling all over the world and winning prizes for her work to staying home and caring for her daughter (a very common choice in Germany, the country that invented the word *rabenmutter*, raven mother, as a derogatory term for women who prioritise their work), and lists what she obtained with the change: 'incontinence, boredom, weight gain, sagging breasts, end of romance, lack of sleep, dumbing down, career downturn, loss of sex drive, poverty, exhaustion, lack of fulfilment'.

Fischer's book, which cost her insults and attacks of all kinds, as well as death threats, is not the only one of its type. As the cult of motherhood has consolidated in our lifetime, our hunger to probe its dark corners has grown, leading to the emergence of an editorial para-industry for highly acclaimed titles like *Regretting Motherhood: A Study*, a book in which Israeli sociologist Orna Donath gathers testimonies from twenty-three women who express feelings similar to those shared by Sophia, a mother of two children between one and four years old:

> I don't want them, and I really don't want them. But they're here. They're here. . . . Even if – God forbid – they die, they will still be with me all the time. Mourning for them, the memory of them, and the pain will be intolerable. To lose them now – of course it would bring some relief.

Modern motherhood, now that the tap to talk and write about it has opened, includes the turbulence as part of the experience of mothering and is keen to explore it. It's great for SEO: Google loves it.

Nevertheless, and despite public appetite for exploring the darker side of the maternal experience, first-person accounts from mothers who leave their children remain infrequent. On Mumsnet, the popular British forum for mums, which has been called a power behind the throne – no candidate on Downing Street can escape being interviewed on Mumsnet – and can generate ideology (for instance, the forum is thought to be responsible for the UK surge in TERFs, proponents of the self-declared 'feminism' that excludes trans women), women start threads about everything from the most frivolous subjects to the most profound, from the decline of the Marks & Spencer design department to advice on tracking ovulation. In Mumsnet's long history, its users have initiated hundreds of thousands of conversations about everything remotely related to motherhood, parenting, and family. But there isn't room for mothers who abandon their children there either. Of all the threads you can consult in its digital archive, there is just one in which a woman announces that she is ready to separate from her husband and is considering leaving him with one of their two children, at least until he digests the news. The women who commented on the post disregarded its central question (what is the best way to leave) and focused on the latter aspect. Every single one of them asked her not to do it. How are you going to choose, they said, with the same contempt with which several Twitter users called for me to die with my cats (I'm terribly allergic, it's not too far-fetched) or lose custody of my children, who were supposedly being deprived of the excellence of Pixar.

Generally on Mumsnet forums, empathy towards the person stating their problem prevails. The site's invisible protocol demands the confessing mother be treated with courtesy from the start, similar to groups like Alcoholics Anonymous. In this

case, however, the protocol went out the window. All the participants aligned like one person, to make it known to this woman,
in the harshest possible terms, that what she was proposing was
heinous and unnatural. They didn't mince their words: having
two children and abandoning one, they said, was completely
beyond comprehension.

With precedent like this, it's unsurprising that there are almost
no stories in first-person on the site about mothers who leave
for reasons outside of violence or economic imperatives. Nor
are there statistics. In Spain, 83 per cent of single-parent homes
are headed by women. The remaining 17 per cent include
widowers, divorced fathers with full custody, and men who have
decided to parent on their own. It must also include some cases
in which mothers have chosen to leave. All of them are bad bad
mothers who, for the moment at least, prefer not to say so.
Their stories remain untold, and no one can find them on the
internet or in libraries, looking for either validation or scandal.

What has emerged is a literature of sad mothers who make
brief trips back to their lives without children, to remember
what they were like. In the beginning they're often accompanied
by the illicit feelings of infidelity, but also a touch of excitement.
In *The Lost Daughter* by Elena Ferrante, Leda abandons her
children for three years to pursue an affair with a university
classmate and resume her academic career. Claire Vaye Watkins
writes in *I Love You But I've Chosen Darkness* about a woman
named Claire Vaye Watkins, a novelist like herself, who leaves
her baby for a year because she wants to 'behave like a man',
'a slightly bad' one. In these stories of errant mothers, there is
no longer any need for the protagonist to travel along a redemp-
tive arc. Yes, there is guilt, a capricious and multifaceted guilt,
which drops in on the sad mother when she is least expecting
it. And some faulty epiphanies. No one discovers anything, no

one learns anything, and the relationships between these 'unnatural' – as Leda puts it – mothers and their children are not peaceful, but nor are they catastrophic. The mud they splash around in is much more lifelike than that.

Gala Dalí and the Matter of the Magnetic Woman™

The magnetic woman's life in practice must be tough to manage. It's hard for the magnetic woman to make friends. The magnetic woman laughs little and out of time, to maintain a sense of mystery. Furthermore, the magnetic woman is condemned to disappoint, since when she finally opens her mouth, she can't possibly measure up to what's expected of her. It's much better if she simply keeps it shut.

Gala Éluard or Gala Dalí or Elena Ivanovna Diakonova was clearly a magnetic woman. Better yet, she was a Magnetic Woman™, one of the fifteen or twenty women inscribed in the twentieth century's historiographic canon, whom people wrote about ceaselessly before journalism and the publishing industry began to take an interest in other women who were less stupendous, less connected, definitely less magnetic.

Often there was talk of her in relation to her husbands. It's curious that in most of her biographies her life begins at seventeen, when she met Paul Éluard, as if her prior infancy and adolescence were mere formalities to prepare her for what they describe, her meeting important men.

More recent works about her, like Estrella de Diego's biography, Monika Zgustová's novelised account, *The Intruder*, and the exhibition the Barcelona Museu Nacional d'Art de Catalunya devoted to her in 2018, titled *A Room of One's Own in Púbol*, go in the opposite direction. All of these readings of the figure of Gala move away from the familiar twentieth-century account; they avoid calling her a 'muse', for example, because we now recognise that as a reductive and patriarchal term, reinstating her as the essential sponsor of her famous partners, a kind of artist without an oeuvre, or an artist who devoted her entire life to perfecting her major work: herself. De Diego, who has studied Gala extensively, goes as far as suggesting that she could be considered a co-author of some of Éluard's work. But even these reinterpretations continue to move within the framework of the Magnetic Woman™. They took away the title of 'muse', but not 'snake charmer'.

Another thing that befalls magnetic women: their status is incompatible with the idea of motherhood. There is nothing more foreign to the idea of a caryatid – there to fascinate, to be observed – than imagining her the subject and devotee of a small human among whose many missions is that of snatching away her shine. There's a reason magnetic women have traditionally only existed in artistic environments or the upper classes, where it's possible to outsource the care of one's children.

There's a beautiful, cruel Dorothy Parker story called 'Horsie' which exposes the dichotomy between the fascinating woman and the normal one. In the story, 'Horsie' is the nickname the Cruger family, a moneyed, fragrant, attractive couple, have given Miss Wilmarth, the night nurse they've hired for a few months to care for their new baby, Diane. Everything Camilla Cruger is – ironic, idle, the kind of person for whom the word 'pout' was invented – poor Horsie is not. One has magnetism in spades, the other has never known it and never will.

Motherhood makes a stealthy lateral appearance in the story, which is actually about the injustice of beauty (the injustice of not having it, essentially), but it gives it another dimension, since the reader can conclude that being magnetic is at odds with being a functional, operative mother, what we understand the phrase 'a good mother' to mean.

In the story, Camilla barely interacts with her baby and avoids holding her, while Nurse Wilmarth takes care of the little one and informs her parents of her progress nightly. She tells them if she has slept, how many ounces she has gained. This information is not met with much interest from her audience. Camilla calls the baby 'useless' and her husband curses the child because she is the reason his wife, who is 'pale as moonlight' and 'had always worn a delicate disdain, as light as the lace that covered her breast', is prostrate in bed, or on her apricot-coloured chaise lounge, and he is obliged to dine nightly with Horsie, whose status within the household is considered too high for her to eat with the cook and the chauffeur.

Nurse Wilmarth's hands are 'big, trustworthy . . . scrubbed and dry, with nails cut short' (the nails of a mother, or a nanny). Camilla's are 'like heavy lilies in a languid breeze'; her nails, a magnetic woman's.

That's one of the many times flowers are mentioned in the story, which reads as if perfumed from start to finish. On her last day in the house, the Crugers gift Horsie a bouquet of gardenias, a cruel joke for their own amusement, since gardenias are the flowers used to crown horses that win a race. Poor Horsie is not in on the joke, of course, and leaves that house happy with her gardenias. The reader knows it will be a very long time, maybe her entire life, before she is given flowers again.

In children's stories there are no mothers who are also magnetic women. In the tales we know from popular folklore, now diffused by Disney and Pixar, there can only be two kinds of mothers, self-sacrificing or dead. The magnetic ones, the vain women who cannot resist their own reflections, are almost always stepmothers. Like Snow White's stepmother, who orders her stepdaughter killed when she begins to surpass her in beauty, or Hansel and Gretel's, who chooses to sacrifice the children that are not hers when there isn't food enough for everyone. Because she lacks the primordial mother gene, sacrifice, she would rather eat than ensure her husband's children can do so.

The fact is, in the original versions of these stories by the Brothers Grimm, those characters were written as mothers, somewhat unnatural mothers. In a piece about her own experience as a stepmother, the writer Leslie Jamison explains that the Brothers Grimm first wrote those fables extracted from folklore in 1812, and then revised them for another edition much later, in 1857. In that second version, many of the cruel, aggressive, and manipulative mothers were converted into stepmothers or mothers by usurpation, as in the case of Rapunzel, who is kidnapped as an infant and raised to believe her captor is her mother. That shift allowed children to maintain the maternal ideal, to concentrate not only evil but also vanity in an external figure, rather than one of their own blood. If these women, already at the upper limit of their reproductive years, have anything in common, it's that they intend to continue seducing the father/husband that triangulates the family, and anyone who stands in their way.

It is likely that Gala, or Elena, had no aspirations to become a mother. In her diary, a slim 106 pages, found in the castle of Púbol in 2004, her only daughter, Cécile, doesn't feature once. She does, however, talk about the rejection she felt when she saw her little sister, Lidia, for the first time, born when Gala was seven years old. 'She was a piece of red flesh, congested, bloated, howling. I felt repulsed when I looked at her.'

Within those pages, Gala also describes the violent abuse she suffered at the hands of one of her brothers, Vadka. When she was a little girl, she writes, Vadka began to pay 'obsessive, irresistible visits, full of that dark, tortured, damned passion' to her room at night. It's interesting, but not surprising, that the revelation of this fact has barely changed the public's view of Gala, and maybe she would have preferred it that way, since her temperament didn't square well with the figure of the victim.

When Gala and Paul Éluard met, no one knew them by those names. He was Eugène Grindel, the adolescent son of a petite-bourgeoisie family in Saint-Denis, his mother a seamstress, his father a real estate agent. She was still Elena. They were both just seventeen years old and had overlapping stays at the Clavadel Sanatorium, near Davos, where their families had sent them to recover from tuberculosis. One day he drew a triangle on a sheet of paper and wrote 'portrait of a young poet'. He passed her the note, and the 'little Russian', as his family would later nickname her, responded: 'Today you shall dine with me.' He told her he wanted to be a poet and that his family opposed the plan; the girl assumed the role of inspiration and critic, the beginning and end of his poems. There's a very famous photo of the two of them in Clavadel, both dressed up as Pierrot for a dance, playing at being twins.

The young couple had to separate in April 1914, three months before all of Europe blew up. Eugène was drafted, although due to his poor health, they assigned him to the rearguard. Even so, he suffered bronchitis, anaemia, and chronic appendicitis and spent almost the entirety of 1915 in a military hospital near Paris. During all that time, the lovers didn't stop sending each other letters and poems. They had a plan. She convinced her mother and stepfather to let her study at the Sorbonne. Surprisingly, they agreed, despite the raging war. From Moscow, with their Swiss housekeeper, she travelled by boat to Helsinki, then moved on to Stockholm, embarked for London, arrived at Southampton, crossed to Dieppe, and reached Paris. The couple married on 21 February 1917, taking advantage of his military leave, and spent the night in a hotel. Weeks later, revolution broke out in Russia, and she could no longer communicate with her family. A little after that, she became pregnant with Cécile, who was born in May 1918. It was rumoured she would have preferred a boy and wanted to name him Pierre.

Isolated, living with her in-laws, and with her poet-husband still on the front, Gala/Elena found motherhood intolerable. When Paul finally returned, her young, tuberculous poet had changed. Now he was an ordinary man, prepared to work in his father's office and become a slightly modified version of his progenitor, carry out a tranquil life in the Parisienne suburbs with his Russian wife and little girl. In *The Intruder*, Monika Zgustová mentions the Russian word 'byt', so short but nevertheless so expressive. 'Byt' encompasses all that is domestic, familiar, material, all that is not 'bytie', spiritual. 'Byt' was everything that young, thirsty woman wasn't interested in. Inside it, Gala also included her daughter, Cécile. How could she separate one from the other when all of it went together: the girl and less poetry, the girl and worse sex, the girl and the tedium of the bourgeois life she thought she had escaped when she married a writer.

Short-term, the solution she found was to share the care of the girl with other women in the family: aunts and Éluard's mother, who ended up raising the child. Still, she didn't have much to do herself, besides encourage her husband to undertake new adventures. Along with André Breton, Louis Aragon, Tristan Tzara, and others, he founded the magazine *Littérature*, and she liked that world, although it wasn't easy for her to win over those intellectuals, who saw her as strange and difficult.

Everything livened up quite a bit in the summer of 1921, when the Éluard family went to Cologne on holiday (without Cécile), to meet Max Ernst. He was married to the art historian Louise Straus, and they had a son, Jimmy, but it wasn't long before he entered into a three-way relationship with Gala and Éluard: a new triangle, just like in Clavadel, but a little more crowded now.

The next summer, the couple again left Cécile with her grandparents and went to Tirol with Hans Arp, Tristan Tzara, and their partners. Max Ernst settled in with the couple and ended up leaving his wife, but Gala didn't feel completely at ease with the arrangement, despite her husband's tranquil acquiescence. When the summer came to an end, the German remained in the Eaubonne villa with the Éluards. Every morning Paul took the train into Paris to work at his father's office, while Max and Gala stayed home, him painting and her watching him, while little Cécile ran around. The transformation of the villa delighted Gala; it no longer looked like it belonged to an insurance broker and housewife, but rather to three polyamorous artists. Ernst painted frescoes on all the walls. A naked woman cut in half, her viscera visible, which terrified Cécile, and above the girl's bed, a duck on wheels. In the master bedroom, huge human hands and aardvarks devouring ants. 'We lived there, all together, quite naturally . . . I don't remember finding it odd,' said Cécile, now an old woman, in an interview in the *Guardian* in 2014. The arrangement lasted a few not-so-harmonious years, during which the surrealists blamed Gala for Éluard's worsening depression. After a trip to Saigon, during which they spent three weeks at the Hotel Casino, Ernst collected his belongings from Eaubonne and departed. He left his frescoes there. Many years later, Cécile and one of her four husbands recovered them, convincing the villa's subsequent owners to strip the painted walls. They asked Ernst to sign them and sold them to Farah Diba, who was building an art collection. Now the testimony of that surrealist lust triangle is on view at the Tehran Museum of Contemporary Art.

After that experience, Paul and Gala went back to functioning as a couple, but not for long. The precarious balance was thrown off again one summer, in 1929, when a young, relatively unknown painter, Salvador Dalí, invited the two to visit him in Cadaqués for a few weeks. This time Cécile did come along, and so did René Magritte and his wife, Georgette, the gallerist Camille Goemans, and his friend Yvonne Bernard. What happened there has been recounted many times. Dalí was struck down by that ephebic woman, who made no effort to come off as likable. She was intrigued by the man who painted women with excrement on their pants. In her fictionalised biography, Zgustová imagines that in one of their first conversations, they talked about Cécile and how, in Gala's mind, the girl was confused with her little sister, that creature who had struck her as so repugnant when she was born. She had wanted a boy and wasn't able to love her daughter as mothers are supposed to. At the end of the summer, Cécile became ill with typhoid fever, which allowed Gala to stay a bit longer at the Miramar Hotel in Cadaqués. Gala, who wasn't used to the role, was impatient when it came to caring for the girl and slipped out for boat excursions with the painter. 'After she met Dalí, she was not interested in me anymore,' Cécile would often say in interviews she gave at ninety-five years old, when the media realised the elderly woman who had once had all the vanguards walking around her living room was still alive. 'She was never very warm, even before. She was very mysterious, very secretive,' Cécile said of her mother in the same *Guardian* interview

That same autumn, they sent the girl to live with her paternal grandmother, who was in reality the one who had looked after her most since she was born. Perhaps the mother thought her daughter would be better off there, since she and Dalí spent their first winter in a former fisherman's hut in Port Lligat, of twenty-five square metres. Maybe she didn't consider it a suitable place for a child. Whatever the truth, very shortly after, Dalí started making money, lots of money. And the couple traded the hut without electricity for room 1610 at the St Regis Hotel in Manhattan, where they spent winters. Tourists crowded at the entrance in hopes of glimpsing the famous moustachioed painter strolling around in a golden cape of dead bees or carrying a box of flies, as the newspapers described.

Nor was there space for Cécile in the universe Gala and Salvador came to inhabit, that of true celebrity, in which a Mickey Mouse might as well be a melting clock. The girl lived with her grandmother and saw her father with relative frequency. She got along very well with Éluard's second wife, Nusch. Mother and daughter only met up about once a year. Money was a source of tension between the child's parents. Paul demanded more from Gala for care of the child, who, to make matters worse, was ordinary, nothing special, barely magnetic, in the eyes of her mother, who herself was increasingly so in the eyes of the rest of the world. When they were together, Gala and Salvador Dalí were a perfect two-headed monster, and they signed some work that way, as if they were one person: Gala Salvador Dalí. On her own, she was a master in image control, suggests Estrella de Diego in her book *Querida Gala*, proposing we consider Gala an artist disguised as a model, a feminine dandy. Neither of these roles – not performer, not dandy – are very well suited to what is traditionally expected of a mother.

There were a couple of unpleasant episodes in the long non-relationship between mother and daughter. In June 1940, while the German army advanced towards Paris, Cécile, who was then twenty-two years old, fled the capital. She knew her mother had rented a villa in Arcachon that summer, fifty kilometres from Bordeaux. The roads were full of people trying to leave Paris and go south. When Cécile arrived there, the domestic worker who opened the door took her for an imposter. She told her the señora did not have a daughter, and as she went to close the door, it occurred to her to confirm the fact with two guests in the house, Man Ray and Marcel Duchamp. After learning that Cécile was indeed Gala's daughter, the employee let her in, and there were the two surrealists, playing chess. She was able to spend a few days at the house in Arcachon while the Nazis invaded Paris.

Many years later, the doors to her mother's house were again closed to Cécile. It was 1983, and she had received notice that Gala, who was eighty-eight, was dying. She went to Port Lligat to visit her for a final time, but the staff, this time allegedly guided by Gala herself, informed her that her mother did not wish to see her, and she had to return to France without saying goodbye. According to Joan Bofill, a Barcelona video artist who has for years been working on a documentary about Cécile Éluard, and who interviewed her many times when she was already quite old, it's not clear if Gala was sufficiently alert to reject her daughter, or if someone else in the house had their own reasons for doing so.

Within the sad story of separation between mother and daughter, there is a seemingly mismatched piece that has been added to the puzzle in recent years. According to the journalist

José Ángel Montañés in his book *The Secret Child of the Dalís*, both the painter and Gala had a very close relationship with another child, Joan Figueras, whom they took under their wing and who spent extensive time in their home. They called him 'Juanett boniquet', precious little Joan, brought him gifts from their travels – on one occasion, Walt Disney gave him baseball gear – and took him on excursions to Barcelona, where they always stayed at the Ritz. In the book, Montañés describes Gala as a loving protectress of this child, who was indeed a boy, as she had wished Cécile to be.

Not even in death did Gala wish to make amends with her daughter. She left her out of her will, and Cécile only received fifty million pesetas and some artwork following Dalí's death because she reached an agreement with the Spanish government. Cécile, who died in August 2016, is buried beside Nusch, her father's second wife. When asked if Nusch had been her second mother, she said no, that such a thing didn't exist. She already had a mother, the worst. In the conversations Bofill had with an elderly Cécile, she showed total admiration for her father, whom she had idealised. Although he, too, in a last-minute gesture, omitted her from his will. With respect to her mother, Cécile always spoke with one dose of resentment and another of distant admiration.

The latter seems to indicate that even her own daughter bought into the magnetic woman mythos surrounding Gala. Almost all of us see our mothers from such a close distance that we can barely make out their contours. They're stuck to us, and it's hard for us to give them magnitude, to keep in mind that they are complex beings as well as mothers. For Cécile, Gala was the complete opposite. She saw her from very far off, so far off that Gala retained what mothers are rarely able to, least of all with their own children: the deceptive machinery of fascination, the mystery. That invention will forever be a sibylline trick, honed to denigrate women while pretending to elevate them. Sometimes it's women themselves who build upon these categories, the Camillas and the Horsies, the magnetic and the demagnetised. Always hoping, of course, to land on the good side.

In my twenties, when life is most expansive and peripheral friendships are most practicable, I spent a significant amount of time with the most Camilla-like girl I had encountered outside of a film. She had carefully crafted her image as someone complex and dark, with difficult relationships and big dilemmas that never allowed her time to deal with anything but herself. Her problems were always a full-time job. When you talked with her, especially if she wasn't trying to seduce you, she would stare half a hand's width above your head, and that's when you knew you had lost her attention, if indeed you had ever had it. My Camilla, with her shoulder-length red hair, even dressed as if she were protagonist in her own noir film, avoiding the fashions of the time, which the rest of us embraced with varying degrees of enthusiasm. At twenty-five, she was already very aware of the cinematographic value of a well-knotted trench coat.

Our friend groups stopped intersecting, and I lost track of her. Much later, I ran into her in the place where I least expected to, one of the day-time festivals where parents take their small children as an excuse to day drink. These events are always well organised. There's always food without allergens for the children, DJ workshops, and people doing face painting. In the morning, music groups for children perform, and in the evening, there are bands the parents enjoyed when they had more dignified social lives.

The main problem with these festivals is that one invariably encounters, in line for a vermouth or waiting to do some children's graffiti activity, faces from another time, faces seen many years before in bars and at concerts, when they had more collagen in their cheeks, firmer skin, shinier pupils. Confirming the collapse of these faces immediately makes you think of the fall of your own, and that, in the end, somewhat dampens the experience of drinking vermouth on a closed-off street with another fifteen hundred exhausted adults and their progeny.

One of those Saturdays – I don't remember if it was in line for the toilet or the stall where you could make your own David Bowie mask, or trying to buy noodles from a truck – I glimpsed my Camilla. She, too, was dragging along a child close in age to the one I was holding right then. How is that possible, I thought. Not her, she wouldn't have got mixed up in all this. It was as if you had told me Gene Tierney was heading up the inclusivity committee at the parent-teacher association, or Barbara Stanwyck knew the words to the songs from *Frozen*. It made absolutely no sense that this magnetic woman, who had made me feel so small in our younger years, would turn up in a place like that. Nevertheless, there she was, without a doubt. Her hair was still shiny, and her cheeks and facial contours retained an admirable elasticity. Sure, she had dark undereye circles, but she covered them up with sunglasses that fell outside current trends, entirely their own thing. She was wearing Oxfords rather than the trainers 90 per cent of the people present had chosen. She didn't see me or acted like she didn't see me, because her son was demanding all her attention, and now, she could no longer stare half a hand's width above his head.

An Ogre, a Princess, an Ass: Mothers Who Leave in Meryl Streep's Career

Since she was canonised by the industry and the public as *the* actor of her generation, Meryl Streep has had the opportunity to do just about everything on screen. She has been a nun, a factory worker, a prime minister, a fashion tsarina, a romance novelist, a rockstar, a witch, a fox (in *Fantastic Mr Fox*), and a mother; many mothers.

She played a mother who is single by choice in *Mamma Mia!*, a sick, cruel mother addicted to pills in *August: Osage County*, an accommodating, multitasking mother who can bake croissants while stoned in the comedy *It's Not That Easy*, and a despised and negligent mother, accused of causing her own baby's death, in *A Cry in the Dark*, a film that depicts the famous Australian story in which a dingo, a wild dog, ate a baby in 1980. The entire country believed the mother had killed the baby because she didn't seem contrite enough on TV, or her sadness wasn't the kind the public demanded. Kate McCann, the mother of Madeleine McCann, was victim of the same prejudice many years later, even though she has never been arrested or charged with any wrongdoing. People wrote articles about the number of times she changed clothes or wore coloured scrunchies while she looked for her missing daughter. A grieving mother, an innocent mother, would never put anything in her hair, several reporters pronounced, along with many self-styled commentators.

Meryl Streep, the mother of cinema, also played a mother who leaves, or is at risk of leaving, her children in three films that polarised audiences when they came out, and that still act as a kind of moral test for viewers today: *Sophie's Choice, Kramer vs. Kramer,* and *The Bridges of Madison County.*

The first, based on a novel of the same name by William Styron, gave Streep an opportunity to again showcase her ability with accents – in this case, Polish – and to present the audience with the kind of dilemma that's thrilling to encounter in fiction, since it allows one to surrender to the perverse game of 'What would I do'. It was met with grave enthusiasm and a certain measure of obligation (the classic combination reserved for Oscar-nominated films).

Both in the novel and the film, we first encounter the character of Sophie, or Zofia, as a non-mother, a single woman living in a guest house in Brooklyn at the start of the fifties. Sophie enters into the classic pre-love triangle with her boyfriend, Nathan, who claims to be a biologist at Pfizer, and the newest guest in the house, the aspiring writer Stingo who also narrates the book and the movie.

Only in the second half of the film do we learn that Sophie had two children she lost in Auschwitz, and we're already nearing its end when she relays to Stingo what actually happened. When they dragged her to the concentration camp, although she was Catholic and the daughter of an antisemitic judge, one Nazi official, a doctor, subjected her to an impossible choice purely for his sadistic enjoyment. Zofia gets off the train along with thousands of other victims, carrying her three-year-old daughter, Eva, in her arms, and holding the hand of her son, Jan. In that moment, the Nazi official makes her an offer: she can choose one of the two of them to go to the camp for children. The other will be taken directly to the gas chamber. If she doesn't make a choice, both will be taken. Initially, she refuses. How could she possibly do that?

But in a matter of seconds, seeing that he does intend to take both her children from her, Zofia makes a decision. She hands the girl over to the Nazi official, who, in a flash, carries her away from her mother forever. In the film, the actor who plays Eva, Jennifer Lawn Lejeune, who was four at the time, howls savagely when they pull her from the arms of Meryl Streep, who had been playing with her for days to earn her trust. Supposedly it was Streep and not the director, Alan J. Pakula, who had the idea of allowing only the cries of the girl to be heard in the scene, and for Streep to limit herself to opening her mouth a few times in a mute grimace. That facial expression, which anyone who has seen the movie recalls, must have been at least 30 per cent of the reason she won an Oscar for the role.

Neither Styron's book nor Pakula's film explains at any point why Sophie chose to hold on to Jan, who also ends up dying in the death camp, and not Eva. The most widespread theory is that the boy was older and stronger and therefore had a greater chance of survival. The decision, useless in the end, since the Nazis end up killing both the boy and the girl, forever brands Sophie's destiny: she survives the Holocaust but not her own conscience and ends up committing suicide.

The person who accompanies her in death is Nathan, who is not, in fact, a biologist but a schizophrenic librarian who carries out a complex operation to victimise and inflict guilt upon Sophie. First he gives her back her life, when he meets her shortly after she arrives in the United States, famished and destroyed, and then he drives her to relinquish it. In one key scene, Nathan, Jewish and obsessed with the Holocaust, tortures Sophie, asking her how she, the Catholic, avoided perishing, what sex work saved her skin.

The feminist reading of *Sophie's Choice*, undertaken in 2001 by a gender studies and literature professor named Lisa Carstens, accuses Styron of revictimising his protagonist, for insinuating Zofia deserved that cruel fate, that she was creating her own problem by responding to the Nazi doctor in perfect German rather than Polish, and trying to bargain with death ('I am not a Jew, neither are my children'). The work, which is closer to popular fiction (it was an indisputable bestseller) than to the small stratum of books considered suitable for academic dalliance, has been analysed much more frequently from the ethnic/religious angle than with regards to what it has to say about motherhood. Cynthia Ozick, for example, reproaches Styron for converting the Holocaust into a human tragedy and not a specifically Jewish one: choosing a Catholic protagonist and thereby robbing Jews of their protagonism in the Shoah.

Little has been written about Sophie as a guilty mother. From the start, it's quite clear that both Styron and, later, Pakula, legitimise the popular intuition that a mother cannot survive the voluntary sacrifice of her child. A natural mother, they conclude, self-castigates with death if she is incapable of saving her children. And the fact that there is a war with a genocide at its centre doesn't substantially change the equation. Sophie was not able to save her children and therefore she believes she also deserves to die.

In the movie, Stingo, who is in love with Sophie, tries to save her. He proposes that they marry and together run the farm he has inherited in Virginia. That's when she has to reveal her tragedy to him. She could never give him children, she says. She doesn't deserve them, because of what she did to little Eva.

A few months after the film premiered, a very pregnant Meryl Streep stepped up to receive her Oscar, and the public, who can never quite overcome their penchant for confusing actors with their roles, felt reassured by that baby bump, that rosy and healthy glow. Everything had turned out OK for the delicate young blonde who was about to have her own child.

It had only been three years since Meryl Streep's last Oscar, which she had received for best supporting actress, for her performance of another mother with a tragic backstory, Joanna in *Kramer vs. Kramer*.

In the hinge between the seventies and the eighties, almost two decades had passed since Betty Friedan published *The Feminine Mystique*, but the narrative of the frustrated wife still had traction in the mainstream. One of the most successful young adult series in the United States, Cynthia Voigt's Tillerman Cycle, which starts with *Homecoming* (1981), opens with a mother who abandons her four children at a gas station. In 1979, the same year *Kramer vs. Kramer* was released, Marianne Faithfull had improbable success with her version of 'The Ballad of Lucy Jordan'. The song tells the story of Lucy, a thirty-seven-year-old suburban mother who lies in bed after taking the kids to school, thinking about how she never drove through Paris in a sports car, with the wind tousling her hair. The last verse, in which a man offers her his hand to help her into a white car, has been interpreted as a suicide, but Faithfull herself has stated that Lucy is actually climbing into an ambulance that will take her to a psychiatric hospital. Lucy has lost her mind trying to live a conventional life.

Joanna Kramer is more worldly than Lucy Jordan. She lives on the Upper West Side, rather than in the neighbourhood filled with white picket fences where we imagine Lucy. And surely she has been to Paris one or several times, maybe on a semester abroad during her years at Smith, reading Baudelaire in cafés and doing those things young Americans do in Paris. But Joanna's problem is essentially the same as Lucy Jordan's, and so is the choice she is given: either go, or go crazy.

It's undeniable that *Kramer vs. Kramer* touched a social nerve when it came out. It was one of the highest grossing films in 1979, alongside hits like *Alien, Rocky II,* and *Apocalypse Now.* The press discussed it on a sociological and generational level. In the more than forty years that have passed since its release, it has continued to generate various readings, some of them contradictory. It has been interpreted as a defence of so-called 'men's rights', which found their standard-bearer in Ted Kramer, the man who, when forced to take care of his son alone, manages as well as any mother. Along those lines, there is an impulse to read *Kramer vs. Kramer* under the banner of antifeminist backlash, a reaction to second-wave feminism, which had been accused of dynamiting the traditional family.

The idea of divorce as a social failure was in the air at the start of the eighties in rich countries. Not in Spain, of course, where it was legalised in 1981 and getting divorced was still seen as modern and aspirational, a subject fit not for dramas but for comedies, like Mariano Ozores's *¡Qué Gozada de Divorcio!* (*What a Fun Divorce!*). In the United States, on the other hand, there was much concerned and sombre writing on the topic of 'latchkey kids', like Elliot and his siblings, the protagonists of *E.T.*, the children of divorced parents who had to open the door to the house with their own key when they got home from school because their mothers weren't there to let them in. Their mothers were working and their fathers were at other homes, maybe with other children already, and less liberated, less distracted new wives.

Kramer vs. Kramer opens when Joanna is on the verge of

leaving Billy. What kind of mother abandons her child? This kind: a svelte blonde in a classic Burberry raincoat who paints clouds in her son's room, so he feels like he's sleeping in the sky. The night she has decided to leave, Joanna tucks Billy in and tells him she loves him. Then she packs a suitcase of essentials and throws in one of his dirty sweaters. When I saw the movie as a mother, I understood instantly why she does this. So she can smell the sweater when the longing becomes unbearable, of course.

Then Ted arrives from drinks with his ad agency boss, euphoric. After five months of effort, he has secured an important account, and they're going to make him creative director. This is supposed to be, he'll say later, one of the five happiest days of his life. In the description of the movie Netflix produced for its menu, they call Ted a yuppy, but that's a bit of a historical misnomer. Firstly, because the word wasn't popularised until 1983, four years later. And secondly, because Ted, with his studied mess of hair, his corduroy trousers, and the vintage advertisements hanging in his office, doesn't fit within the stereotype as we now understand it. Ted is clearly a Democrat, a child of the sixties who, for whatever reason, didn't find the time to include feminism in his ideological overhaul.

Joanna tries to tell him repeatedly that she's really going, but Ted doesn't listen. She leaves the keys and the dry-cleaning tickets and warns him that she is serious. Already in the lift, Joanna explains to her husband that if she doesn't, she'll end up jumping out a window, and that she's not taking the child with her because lately she hasn't been good to him; she's impatient. Then Ted, incredulous, is alone in the flat with his son, probably for the first time since he was born.

After that, we lose sight of Joanna until the last third of the movie, when she returns from California remade, with blue eyeshadow, a therapist, and a good job. There's plenty that is reactionary in the film, but here is a detail that should draw half a smile from any feminist accustomed to reading news about pay inequity: Ted ends up losing his job as an advertising executive because of the many hours he is dedicating to his son, and the very day he is fired, he gets another job where he makes five thousand dollars less a year. His wife, newly returned to the job market after six years of parenting, now has a higher salary than he does. The economic penalty for being a mother has shifted from her to him, since he is now the one caring for the child.

The bulk of the movie is for Ted and Billy. The former goes from being the kind of father who doesn't know what grade his son is in (he has to ask at the school gates) to being the kind of father who memorises his child's lines for the school play. This transition, from absent-minded to attentive, is metaphorised in the famous French toast, which Ted isn't able to make for breakfast on their first morning alone but which, over the course of eighteen months, they come to prepare together in silence, like a duo performing a routine in perfect harmony. Eggs, milk, bread, butter, frying pan.

The storyline in which 'man takes responsibility for the care of small children' was enormously profitable in eighties popular cinema, approached from every kind of angle, in every register, which indicates that it was still sufficiently shocking to be the subject of a movie, but at the same time was plausible enough. In fact, Al Pacino rejected the role of Ted Kramer, which in the end went to Dustin Hoffman, because he had already agreed to star in *Author! Author!*, the title of which, in Latin America, was translated as *¡Qué buena madre es mi padre!* (*What a Good Mother My Father Is!*), about a man whose wife grows distant – another mother who leaves – and places in his care not just their son, but four children from her previous marriages.

In 1983, Michael Keaton had notable success with *Mr. Mom*, in which he plays an automotive engineer who has to stay home with the kids when he gets fired and his wife finds a job before he does. And a little later came *Three Men and a Baby*, in which three successful bachelors, successful enough to pay for a huge penthouse right next to Central Park, are forced to take care of one's daughter when her mother leaves her at their doorstep. The explanation the film gives is that the mother lacks the money to care for her, and her decision is barely regarded as a problem. It's an eighties comedy, and somebody has to take care of the baby.

The movie, a remake of the French film with an identical plot called *Trois hommes et un couffin*, premiered in the United States the week of Thanksgiving in 1987 and had extraordinary success. In my home, it was one of the most well-loved movies we had on VHS, along with the sequel, *Three Men and a Little Lady*. I also saw *Kramer vs. Kramer* as a little girl, on TV, with nobody around, drawn in by the idea of a movie about adults getting divorced, highest on the list of subjects I was interested in then, since my parents had also done it. I don't remember much about that viewing, except that I cried a lot, that I felt a little like Billy, and that I didn't understand the ending. I probably wished the parents would get back together, as they did in my favourite movie, *The Parent Trap*, the Hayley Mills version, not the Lindsay Lohan one.

In the end, Joanna Kramer goes back to New York, transformed into, as she puts it, 'a whole human being'. That's when the trial that gives the movie its title takes place, the trial for custody of Billy. Both the lawyers play dirty. Joanna's recriminates Ted for losing his job, and Ted's recriminates Joanna, obviously, for having been able to leave her child.

Despite the fact that at that point she was not yet the

superstar she would soon become, Meryl Streep intervened in the script and wrote herself the crucial monologue of the movie, which was not in the original screenplay and which very likely resulted in her first Oscar. This is an essential episode in what has become 'the legend of Meryl'. When the actress read the Avery Corman novel the movie is based on, she thought Joanna seemed like 'an ogre, a princess, an ass', according to a later interview. She accepted the role only on the condition that she be given some profundity, a reason for abandoning the child beyond merely being the spring that sets off a moral fable in which an egotistical man discovers what is authentic in life.

The director, James Benton, had written the monologue, in which Joanna must convince the judges to return Billy to her care, as a kind of feminine version of Shylock's soliloquy in *The Merchant of Venice* ('If you prick us, do we not bleed?'): 'Just because I'm a woman, don't I have a right to the same hopes and dreams as a man? Don't I have a right to a life of my own? . . . Is my pain any less just because I'm a woman?' Benton suspected, and Streep confirmed, that this was the kind of text a man would write for a woman, not the kind a woman would write for herself, and she proposed to touch it up. The following day, when they filmed, Streep acted the words that she herself had written.

In the monologue, she acknowledges that to leave her son was a terrible thing to do, but that she felt it was the only thing she could do; that she needed to become a whole human being in order to care for him. She pleads with the courtroom that while Billy might need his father, he needs his mother more. The final words of the speech act as an appeal to authority, ending with a masterful repetition: I'm his mother. I'm his mother. What more is there to say? In *Aftermath*, the book in which she writes about her divorce, the author Rachel Cusk, who does not resemble Joanna Kramer at all, employs a similar argument to explain why she and not her husband, who left his job to care for their daughters, should have custody of the girls. 'They're my children, they belong to me,' she tells her ex as her only explanation. 'Call yourself a feminist,' her ex says with all the spite the recently separated can project in only four words.

'Men and women are different, after all. Being a mother isn't the same as being a father,' wrote Marguerite Duras, who never wanted to be a mother, in *Practicalities*. 'Motherhood means that a woman gives her body over to her child, her children; they're on her as they might be on a hill, in a garden; they devour her, hit her, sleep on her; and she lets herself be devoured, and sometimes she sleeps because they are on her body. Nothing like that happens with fathers.'

That's what Joanna Kramer is getting at too. Her soliloquy contains some of the same idea, that a mother is always something different from a father, and the judge understands that without having to have read Marguerite Duras. It's easy for him to join in the age-old entente that recognises children as belonging to their mothers, and he chooses to grant her custody.

Nevertheless, the final scene of the movie offers a twist, devised to give the viewer a satisfying ending. Let's keep in mind that since the beginning, this has been Ted Kramer's story much more than it has been Joanna's, or even Billy's. The day comes when the child is supposed to move in with his mother. The viewer has already swallowed the bitter pill of hearing him ask his father who will read his stories, where his toys will be. Ted and Billy are waiting for Joanna, silent and sad, suitcases packed.

Then Joanna shows up, quite shaken, and asks to talk to her ex-husband alone. She says she has changed her mind. That she thought she should have painted clouds in her flat so Billy would feel like he was at home when he woke up, and then she realised that Billy already has a home, and he should stay there. 'I love him very much,' she says, sobbing. Joanna is still a mother who leaves, now forever, although she will see her son on weekends and half the holidays. Yes, she loses her son, but her reputation is saved, because the movie tries hard to clearly convey that Joanna is making a sacrifice for Billy's own good, even if it is Billy himself that she's sacrificing. It's a masterful, paradoxical move. The character of Joanna retains the essence of traditional motherhood, which is the renouncing of one's own priorities. Only in this case, the priority is the child. And that's how Joanna, in spite of being a mother who leaves – two times, in fact – gains the favour of the audience.

Streep in the cinema left her children again many years later, in one of her more minor films, *Ricki and the Flash*, directed by Jonathan Demme and written by Diablo Cody. Here, the actress, now seventy-six years old, plays Ricki/Linda, a woman who abandons her husband and three children and the conventional life she leads with them in a suburb of Indianapolis to devote herself to music. She half achieves this: she plays with her band at various dive bars, but only when she's not working at her grocery-store cashier job. Many years later, her older daughter, Julie, suffers a nervous breakdown when her marriage fails, and Ricki's ex-husband, portrayed by Kevin Kline, asks her to come back. As one would expect, the three children, now adults, receive their dissident mother with rebukes and a range of emotions, from scorn to indifference. The fact that Julie is played by Streep's eldest daughter, Mamie Gummer, who was a clone of her mother at that age, adds a metatextual layer to the film. For reasons that are difficult to grasp, Meryl Streep's four children, three of whom are, crucially, daughters, decided to pursue careers in film, surely knowing that nothing good could come of it, since the public would inevitably compare them with their mother, their faces conjuring hers.

But *Ricki and the Flash* is not the Merylverse movie that demands to be compared to *Kramer vs. Kramer*. The opposite of Joanna Kramer is Francesca Johnson, the protagonist of *The Bridges of Madison County*. There are only sixteen years between the two films. In the life of a male actor, sixteen years is not long enough for a paradigm shift. If you're Tom Cruise, you still play saviours of humanity who dangle from unlikely places. If you're Paul Giamatti, men with some kind of neurosis and at least one Jewish grandfather. In the case of a female actor, however, even one named Meryl Streep, those sixteen crucial years that take you across your thirties mean you will no longer be cast as the young, desirable mother, like Joanna, but instead as the menopausal matriarch whose life is slipping through her fingers like sand.

Francesca was a war bride, an Italian who met her GI – in this case, a Richard – when the US Army arrived in Bari, married him, and consequently had to spend the rest of her life on a farm in Madison County, Iowa. There, she does what is expected of her. She maintains a pristine kitchen, cooks dinner while listening to opera (the detail Clint Eastwood, the film's director, uses to communicate to us that deep down, this farmgirl is culturally unsettled), and takes care of her teenage children. Until one weekend when she's home alone because the rest of the family is at the state fair, and Eastwood arrives in the form of Robert Kincaid, a divorced and very worldly *National Geographic* photographer who turns the tap of her desire back on.

Over the course of four days, Francesca and Robert live out a romance in miniature: they meet, they fall in love, they sleep together, they fight – 'So, do you want more eggs or should we just fuck on the linoleum one last time?' she says, throwing his portless-sailor act in his face, and it has to be one of the best twenty lines of Meryl Streep's career – they make known that they are the loves of each other's lives. When the return of her husband and children draws near, Francesca's dilemma is laid out on the kitchen table. To leave or not to leave. If she leaves her husband and goes to Italy as Robert is asking her to, she'll also have to renounce her children, though they don't come up often in their discussions, since that would derail the romantic drama, would smudge what wants to present itself as a simple but impossible quandary. The farmer or the photographer.

In fact, the entire film, based on the bestseller by Robert James Waller, is narrated from the point of view of Francesca's children, who, after her death, find letters in which she tells them the story, using that idyll as a source of advice for their own threatened marriages. Not content to keep the Gary Cooper role all to himself, Eastwood infuses those traces of unreformed masculinity his cinema is well known for into Francesca's son, Michael, who at first dismisses his mother as an insolent adulteress when he finds out about her romance three decades after the fact. 'I feel . . . like she cheated on me, not Dad . . . When you're the only son, you sort of feel . . . your mother shouldn't want sex anymore because she has you,' he says calmly. While her daughter is surprised to learn that her mother was the Anaïs Nin of the cornfields.

Just as in *Kramer vs. Kramer*, the central question is that of renunciation. The emotional climax of the movie isn't the first kiss, nor the first time Robert and Francesca sleep together, but the ending, when he says goodbye to her in the rain and she, holding back sobs, doesn't open the door of her husband's car, but remains inside, feet buried forever in the county of Madison, Iowa, with her quiet farmer husband and two children. Francesca at least has the generosity not to make her children pay for her sacrifice. On the contrary, once dead, she seems to be telling them: don't do the same thing I did.

Ultimately, the filmography of this woman, who has spent half a century defining middlebrow taste – a Meryl Streep movie will often be simultaneously good, successful, and commercial – paints quite a depressing image of motherhood. Observing Francesca, Ricki, Zofia, and Joanna, those ogres, princesses, asses, you deduce that the only way to win as far as the mum thing goes is by losing. And it's clear that renunciation lies at the core of acceptable motherhood. The renunciation of a son, as in *Kramer vs. Kramer*; of oneself, as in *Ricki*; of sex and love, as in *The Bridges of Madison County*. Or of one's own life, as in *Sophie's Choice*.

Off-screen, on the other hand, Streep seems to lead a life blessed by balance and equilibrium. A life divorced from any dilemma. Shortly after overcoming the tragedy of losing her partner, actor John Cazale, when she was twenty-nine years old and he was forty-two, the actress met the sculptor Don Gummer. As the story goes, she was forced out of the flat she had shared with him in New York, and on the day she was leaving, her brother came to help her with the move. He showed up with a friend named Don. Six months later, Meryl and Don got married in her parents' backyard. The pair stayed together for forty-five years, always topping the lists of the most stable couples in Hollywood, until they quietly confirmed their separation in 2023. Streep was able to give birth to four children in a row during the most successful decade of her career, and her friend Viola Davis says that when she bakes apple pie, she doesn't buy pre-made dough but makes it by hand instead, because, of course, she's Meryl Streep.

Artisanal Motherhood

Years ago, before I had children, I met a woman who had a son as well as a very demanding job. She lived in the suburbs, and it took her fifty-plus minutes to get to work, carrying her lunchboxes, plural. The breakfast one, the lunch one, and something to snack on mid-afternoon so she wouldn't fall prey to the vending machines at the office. Cut fruit and two little rice cakes in a plastic container with a circular lid.

In total, this woman was spending eleven or twelve hours away from home on workdays. When she got back in the evening, her son was already asleep, and she told me she'd get in bed with him and hug him and sleep there too, hoping the time she spent with the dozing boy counted for something; that if someone were keeping score, they would give her a quarter point for maternal presence for each hour she spent lying next to him, experiencing several levels of discomfort in a twin bed topped with Winnie the Pooh sheets, breathing in that warm vapour children give off at night.

At that time, it seemed to me everything in this woman's life was going badly, that she was mismanaging all of it, and that in two months, she would have a stroke. It's likely I said something along those lines to a friend, with the arrogance of those without children when they judge other people's parenting.

I was totally wrong. The woman hung on in that job for several years as it became increasingly maddening, until she was promoted to a position of even greater responsibility, and also, at over forty, she had another son.

I never had another conversation that frank with her, so I don't know if she's still cuddling up with the elder child at night, if she's now doing that with the younger one, or if she has quit the habit, which no longer strikes me as foreign or tragic, but instead seems like something I might do at any time.

I now speak the same language as that woman, I understand that psychosis and subscribe to it. I've become frustrated and got off city buses that seem too slow, considered other options (a taxi? running down the street like someone who has lost her mind?) that might allow me to scrape together three or seven extra minutes with my children, having spent all day outside the house; I've cried in hotel rooms on work trips when I've realised it's too late to FaceTime the kids, who are asleep in their own time zone on the other side of the world. Five minutes after that moment of sadness and exasperation, I've also felt a burst of pleasure, like the instant effect of a muscle relaxant, at the prospect of being alone in a hotel room, in a dressing gown, without having to make dinner for the kids. A night without putting the broccoli in the steamer at 7.50, a night without beating eggs for tortilla at 8.02, a night without negotiating the application of shampoo and its subsequent rinsing, always a challenge, around 8.42.

Almost all the steamrolled mothers I'm surrounded by go about striving to accomplish the absurd: do their jobs, protect what remains of their emotional lives, and hand-tailor that artisanal motherhood we believe is so desirable. Our version of motherhood, we tell ourselves, should be like the ugly organic carrot, morally superior to the carton of pre-cut fruit. It should be like homemade baby food. It shouldn't be industrial or canned.

All of us are constantly running a mental app we could call the quality-time calculator. It's more or less a currency converter, but for hours and minutes. If someone who understands both software and sociology wanted to develop the app for Android and Apple, it would go something like this: every minute spent with the child doing nonessential activities (meaning that feeding them, changing nappies, etcetera, don't count, or count less) generates a score, which can be higher or lower depending on whether screens are involved. Screens take away points. But there's variation among them. Everyone knows a movie is worth more than a cartoon, a Ghibli movie worth more than a Pixar one, a Pixar movie worth more than one cranked out by Illumination, and so on. *Paw Patrol* probably deducts points.

In this app, everything that reinforces the bond between mother and child and stimulates the child's emotional well-being gives you points: make muffins: 2.5 points. Do a puzzle: 3 points. Paint with watercolours: 4. Draw with crayons: 2.5. The most ambitious mothers might unlock achievements like, 'Write a two-person play with the child and perform it with marionettes made of felt and sustainably sourced wood.'

With the points you earn, you can do two things. The first is privately revel in the conviction that you're not doing such a bad job; better, at least, than the mother of Mateo in year five. And the second is to redeem them for hours spent working or doing activities of your own, during which the care of the child will be externalised to other humans or screens, depending on the household's available balance.

An app like this would only make neat and tidy the calculations we're already doing all the time, and which sometimes lead us to situations that are difficult to explain. In the economy of quality time, the quality of the mother's time is always trending downward.

Like many freelancers, I work most Sunday evenings. If I'm really on top of things, make lunch early, barely sit at the table afterwards reading the paper, avoid watching half a movie, manage to make it to the computer around four, and am able to finish the weekly article I usually deliver to my editors, I might still have a little time with my children, right at the end of the evening, before I make dinner and put them to bed. That situation is close to ideal, according to the mental app I designed and haven't managed to delete. Although it would be more ideal if I could write an article and a half, or two articles. Send invoices. Make oatmeal-and-walnut cookies the kids can snack on all week long. But if you want to succeed with the app, it's important to make modest goals.

One of those Sundays, I managed to add in some time at the swings, almost at twilight, the park completely empty, because the normal parents in my neighbourhood – the salaried ones with weekends – take their kids to the swings during the day, not at night. While I was there, I texted a friend, another steamrolled, guilty mother whom I met through my elder child. Her job is much more serious than mine. We're talking about a successful, respectable person. My friend was on her way back from a weekend at her mother's house, weighed down with several suitcases and bags and pulling her daughter along. When I told her we were at the park at night, it seemed like a normal idea to her, even a great one. She decided to come by for a while, too, though she didn't feel like it in the slightest. 'I have to do some work later. If we come to the park now and the kids play for a while, she'll at least have done some socialising, right?' she asked me in complete seriousness. I confirmed that this would indeed count as socialising for her daughter, who is an only child. Her mother, my friend, feels extra guilt over the ghost siblings she hasn't given her. Those twenty minutes at the park at night would doubtless exonerate her of the crime she was planning to commit by working later, and more than that, by depriving the girl of her full attention.

So the two of them, mother and daughter, showed up at the park with their wheeled carry-ons, the exhaustion of extended travel by bus, and a raffia bag full of leftovers the grandmother had put in Tupperware. Why doesn't this woman go home, put down her bags, make her daughter a sandwich, and get to work? What need does she have to watch her daughter slip down the slide at the park in the remnant-hours of the silliest day of the week?

That's what someone reasonable would think, someone without children of her own, like the person I was when I thought the woman who only saw her son while he was sleeping was doing it all wrong. Adding up points is what you do, pre-emptively pardoning yourself on Sunday for all the motherly misbehaviour you will most certainly carry out over the course of the rest of the week, walking the tightrope of work and care and trying not to tumble off, doing everything a little badly, saying goodbye to your dignity.

Ingrid Bergman: A Daily Sadness

It's not often that a family separation ends up becoming a matter of the state. But this wasn't a typical family. In 1949, Ingrid Bergman wrote the now famous letter to Roberto Rossellini, lighting the fuse of their romance long before they had seen each other in person. Now, it reads as if Bergman wrote it knowing even then that it would be reproduced a thousand times. It's succinct, compact. It's made of the kind of material that would qualify for an Instagram quote. It is the definitive groupie letter, and an appeal to the vanity of a man like Rossellini, who, after receiving it, had no choice but to (a) devise a film for the woman, (b) leave his wife, and (c) leave his lover, none other than Anna Magnani. In the note, not much longer than a telegram, Bergman playfully sells herself as a Swedish actress who gets by in English and German, but can only say 'ti amo' in Italian. She's ready to come and work with Rossellini.

In a surge of increasingly intimate letters, Rossellini and Bergman prepared *Stromboli*, the film they would shoot together on the island of the same name. She would play Karin, a Lithuanian woman who marries a fisherman from the Aeolian Islands to escape the internment camp where she has been held following World War II.

While filming, Ingrid and Roberto fell in love, or, more

precisely, cemented what they had begun by mail. She asked her husband, the Swede Petter Lindström, for a divorce, also in a letter, and he refused. While their tense negotiation was underway, Ingrid became pregnant by Rossellini, and he forbade her from returning to the United States for fear of losing her. In the middle of the dispute was Pia, the ten-year-old girl who had stayed behind while her mother made her Italian movie, whom Ingrid would not see again for two years. After that, they saw each other very sporadically, on uncomfortable visits organised by Petter, which took place in hotels in London. Pia, who as an adult became a journalist, described them as awkward and difficult.

While that drama unfolded in her home, the story of her mother's adultery took on unimaginable dimensions. The media – led by Louella Parsons, the evil queen of Hollywood gossip – eviscerated the Swedish star, whom people thought of as a saint, like Joan of Arc, or a refugee, like the one she played in *For Whom the Bell Tolls*. In March 1950, a democratic senator from Colorado, Edwin C. Johnson, a moralist who had opposed the politics of Franklin D. Roosevelt's New Deal, took up the matter in the US Congress:

> Mr. President, now that the stupid film about a pregnant woman and a volcano [*Stromboli*] has exploited America with the usual finesse . . . are we merely to yawn wearily, greatly relieved that this hideous thing is finished and then forget it? I hope not. A way must be found to protect the people in the future against that sort of gyp.

Johnson proposed a law that made the Hays Code look puny, according to which movies would be approved for licences based on the morality of their directors and leads. He also added, hoping to cash in with his most conservative constituents, that Ingrid Bergman had 'perpetrated an assault upon the institution of marriage', and called her 'a powerful influence for evil'.

All that for breaking up a marriage? Hollywood had been through worse scandals, starting with Errol Flynn and Charles Chaplin's taste for sleeping with, and in Chaplin's case marrying, minors – his successive wives were sixteen, sixteen, twenty-six, and eighteen on their wedding days – and that same year, 1949, another star of similar stature to Bergman, Rita Hayworth, had also started an affair with a married man, Prince Ali Salman Aga Khan, and had married him when she got pregnant, as Ingrid herself would soon do. But Hayworth's image had been hypersexualised by *Gilda*, and although her romance generated some headlines, she was able to carry on with her career more or less as she had before.

Pia Lindström herself, in an interview with Larry King and in the documentary *Ingrid: In Her Own Words*, gives a plausible enough explanation for why her mother had such an effect on the US public, and why they took her actions personally. 'She left for an Italian director. And I think Hollywood felt: after all we've done for you? You know, we've given you a career, we've given you all of this, and now you just turn up your nose and say, I don't like America, and I'm going to live in Italy.' Public opinion had made its own mental sketch of the Swedish actress, a European star whom they found relatable and earthly despite her beauty. They liked the story told in magazines about her marriage to a Swedish doctor with a serious look about him, far removed from glittery spectacle. They had met in Stockholm in 1933, when she was eighteen and he was twenty-five and had recently received his doctorate in dental surgery. They married in 1937, and one year later, Pia was born. When David O. Selznick offered Ingrid a contract in Hollywood, Petter encouraged her to go, and stayed in Sweden with their daughter for a few months until they could be reunited. They were projecting a tolerably modern Scandinavian image. In retrospect, that first trip Ingrid took without her daughter was an early indication that she would be tackling motherhood in her own way.

The reality is, in the home she shared with Petter, Bergman felt 'a daily sadness', as she put it in her diary. The actress kept journals all her life, in part because she was convinced from a very young age that she would do something that mattered, that all the world would one day know her name. Bergman had one of those curious prose styles that benefit from the short-circuits of the multilingual mind. 'A daily sadness' is either a carefully crafted turn of phrase, or the happy accident of someone writing in her second language. A daily sadness is not the same thing as an everyday sadness.

Lindström was already showing evidence of a pronounced Calvinist streak that made him suspicious of pleasure and luxury, and he was very severe with Ingrid. Four years before she wrote her letter to Rossellini, the actress had an affair with the photographer Robert Capa. After that, she had gone back to Lindström, bought and set up a home in Los Angeles, filmed *Notorious* and *Joan of Arc*. But she was disillusioned with her harsh domestic life and what the American film industry could offer her. 'I never understood the kind of happiness I was longing for,' the actress says in the documentary.

The problem with falling in love by superposition, when one is already mired in another relationship, is that the ecstasy is always accompanied by an almost identical dose of pain. While she was filming *Stromboli* and realising with Rossellini all they had anticipated in their letters and telegrams, Bergman continued to feel her dose of 'daily sadness', above all when she thought about Pia. 'It was absolute hell . . . I cried so much I thought there wouldn't be any tears left . . . I felt the newspapers were right. I was an awful woman, but I had not meant it that way,' she says in the film.

What's unusual about this story is that almost everyone involved wrote or talked about the subject extensively in interviews, including Petter Lindström, who, according to his daughter, always felt like an object of public scorn and never completely recovered from Ingrid's betrayal, not even after marrying another doctor, with whom he had four children. The wound the actress had inflicted on his pride never healed

He and Pia stayed in the house in Benedict Canyon. As an adult, the daughter shows an admirable understanding, describing her mother's departure without the bitterness you'd expect, in Ingrid Bergman's 1980 autobiography *My Story:* 'A whole new life opened for her which was dramatic and glorious and a passionate love affair so romantic and glorious. Well, that was grand for Mother. But on the other hand, what was left behind was not. I was part of what was left.'

Meanwhile, Ingrid wrote to the filmmaker Jean Renoir subtly requesting that he intervene.

Maybe you, Jean, whose life, I'm sure, has been difficult, confusing and tossed like a shipwreck, maybe you can explain to Petter that sometimes people leave and they don't go back. The trouble is I don't feel sinful. I'm unhappy so that it almost breaks my heart for what Pia must go through, and also Petter, though he could have helped and finished this thing earlier.

Ingrid and Pia met again when the girl was eighteen, against the wishes of her father, who for years had been telling anyone who would listen, including his own daughter, that the actress was an alcoholic and a bad mother. By then, Ingrid was already divorcing Rossellini, who couldn't understand that she wanted to fully resume her career – curiously, he would only allow her to work with him or Jean Renoir. The family was on the verge of blowing up again and putting itself back together in a new pattern.

Roberto left for India to film a movie, and there, he quickly found a third wife, Sonali Dasgupta. Ingrid went to Paris with her new boyfriend, the Swede Lars Schmidt. And the three children from their marriage, Robertino and twins Ingrid and Isabella, stayed in Rome in the care of various nannies and their stepsister, Pia, whom they hardly knew. After a very early marriage that quickly dissolved, Pia didn't hesitate to set up her life in Europe and care for her three half siblings, though she could just as easily have genuinely resented them, since her mother had given them all the time and attention that Pia lacked. Ingrid's move to Paris set the four siblings on equal footing: they were all fated to carry out relationships with their absent mother by phone, and to see her only occasionally.

The battle for custody of the Rossellini-Bergman children was as bloody as the one Ingrid and Petter had fought over Pia, but as adults, all the children expressed an appreciation for the extra familial scaffolding they had at their disposal: the stabilising presence of that encore father, Lars Schmidt, and their extra mother, Sonali Dasgupta.

The life of Sonali Dasgupta opens a parallel chapter in this story of love, adultery, and serial abandonment spanning three continents. Sonali, who counted Prime Minister Nehru as a childhood friend, was married to the filmmaker Harisadhan Dasgupta when she met Rossellini. She was twenty-seven years old and had two children, one six and the other eleven months. To the outrage of Bengali society, she left her husband, secretly married Rossellini, and went to Europe, taking with her their younger son, Arjun, who would come to be known as Gil. The elder, Raja, she left behind in India with his father. After the death of his mother in 2014, Raja said that he felt no spite towards her, but nor was he going to miss her, just as she had never longed for him.

The successive Bergman-Rossellini-Dasgupta romances led to divorces that first made children motherless and then gave them adoptive mothers, creating an interesting chain of non-traditional motherhoods. Sonali was very close with the three Rossellini children, even after the director left her for another woman sixteen years into their marriage. That unusual experience, of children who have lost their parents for a time but found others along the way, produced very different levels of resentment in everyone affected. On one end of the spectrum is Pia Lindström, who represents total forgiveness, the absence of ill will: the daughter who comes the moment she's asked to help the mother who abandoned her take care of her new children. On the other end is Raja Dasgupta, Sonali's eldest son, the son chosen to stay behind, who would never again see his mother, nor forgive her. Between one story and the other lie almost all the states that might come to pass when a mother chooses to leave.

This saga of love, spite, and cinema is ripe for political-sentimental interpretation. One can choose to read it as a sordid Houellebecqian fable, a diatribe against free love that warns of what happens when adult egotism mows down children's interests. On the other hand, it could be a defence of reconstituted families, untethered filial love. Evidence that children and their parents can choose how to love one another, too, just as couples do. It all depends on whose statements are taken into account, and what one's intention is in telling the story.

In 1978, when all these children were already adults, Ingrid Bergman accepted the role of Charlotte, the pianist in *Autumn Sonata*. It was her first time working with another Bergman, Ingmar, as well as one of his exes, Liv Ullmann. Apparently, Ingrid secured the part the same way she had her role in *Stromboli* three decades before. While in Cannes in 1973, she slipped a note to her countryman and namesake, reminding him he had promised her a role one day. In perfect alignment with the urbane perversity Ingmar Bergman is known for, he remembered that note five years later, just as he was conceiving the role of Charlotte, a successful pianist and bad mother (*bad* bad mother, of course), who, over the course of a single night, is faced with a slew of reproaches from her daughter.

The director said he considered no other actress for either role, they were always Ingrid Bergman and Liv Ullmann in his mind. He didn't explain why – he didn't have to. The mother and daughter in the film haven't seen each other for seven years. Eva, the daughter, who also plays the piano, though without flair or mastery, has a long list of rebukes for her mother, because with Ingmar Bergman, you never get just one drama: she neglected her as a child, along with her sister, Helena, who suffers from a degenerative disease and has been confined to a hospital for years; she left home for eight months, for an affair. Charlotte also never met Erik, Eva's son, who drowned just before he turned four. There are photos of the boy all over the house, reminding both Charlotte and the viewer that an unendurable tragedy took place there.

Eva recriminates her mother for not turning up when her grandson was born – curiously, she doesn't mention her absence from his funeral. 'I was recording all the Mozart sonatas and concertos. I was so busy,' her mother responds. More than one critic has pondered what inspired Ingmar Bergman to write about this dynamic – he had nine children with his five wives, boasted of never knowing their ages, and once said 'I measure the years by my movies, not by my offspring.' Charlotte follows suit, linking her family memories to whatever she was playing at that moment: Mozart, Bartok, Beethoven.

There's a moment when the film turns into an Olympics of suffering, and the daughter's criticisms become as fantastical as her mother's sins. Eva blames her for having caused Helena's illness because Helena fell in love with one of Charlotte's lovers and their mother didn't want to share him. If there's one thing Ingmar Bergman's movies make clear, it's that fights between lovers and parents and children don't always follow impeccable logic.

The relationship between the two Bergmans wasn't an easy one. 'Ingmar, the people you know must be monsters,' Ingrid would say, arguing for a less terrible, more human Charlotte. The actress begged the director to let her include a joke or two in her lines – denied – and to change the seven years she had gone without seeing her daughter to five. Ingmar agreed to the latter at first, but in the final version, it was seven again.

While they were filming, Ingrid was already sick with the cancer that would kill her, and her daughter, Isabella, has described how her left arm would swell up terribly. So as not to appear on screen with one unnaturally swollen arm, the actress would sometimes stay up all night, hanging that arm in the air. According to Isabella, Ingrid saw no reflection of herself in Charlotte, nor had she herself ever felt the resentment and anger of Liv Ullmann's character.

'You know, we never actually lived with our mother, anyways. It was sort of an odd thing. She always chose another country to live in. . . . When we were all in New York, she lived in London,' Pia says, smiling alongside her two half-sisters, without any apparent drama, on *Larry King Live* in 2017. In the documentary *Ingrid Bergman in Her Own Words* and all the interviews the three daughters granted – the son, Robertino, turned up less frequently – they seem to genuinely appreciate the time their mother gave them, knowing she felt called by her profession, and they express an understanding that she wasn't like other mothers.

'We didn't see her that much. But when she was with us, she was wonderful,' Isotta Rossellini said in the same interview, speaking for the three sisters. '[My parents] were the greatest people in the world. . . . they died when we were very young, and we didn't have the chance to have a relationship with them as older people, you know, not as children,' she added, showing either that she has a superior degree of insight and generosity, or she has spent a lot of money on good therapy. Ingrid's children absolve her of her successive abandonments, and she was probably never completely abandoned by her dose of daily sadness, the melancholic's congenital illness.

Watching the Ingrid Bergman documentary brought out my own contradictions again. If I think about the uproar her story of adultery provoked in 1950, it's quite easy for me to put myself on the right side of history. Damn puritans, I might think comfortably, almost effortlessly. But even so, I can't help but recall little Pia Lindström, feeling, as she put it, 'part of what was left'. I also try to imagine the powerlessness of Ingrid herself, a transplant in a country so different from her own, with a husband as difficult as Rossellini was known to be, separated from her daughter and barely able to work, unable to grow her obvious ambition.

Ingrid Bergman's second partial abandonment, when she took up residence in Paris and left all of her children in a flat in Rome under the care of nannies, surprised me perhaps even more than her first divorce. This is, most likely, a reflection of my provincial background. If I had been born into another social class, that kind of arrangement would seem normal to me.

The first work trip I went on after the birth of my elder son, when he was only three months old, consisted of taking a very short plane ride and sleeping away from home for one night. I could have said no to the magazine that had offered it, traded it for an article that I could write at home, but at that point I was very determined to prove I was the same as I'd been before, and I didn't want them to stop considering me for interviews and articles that required travel. I had no desire to be apart from the infant who up until very recently had basically been another internal organ, but I was also enticed by the idea of a short excursion to my pre-mother life. What's more, a luxurious trip, the kind reporters are sometimes granted to spy on worlds we don't belong to in order to describe them for our readers, who probably haven't visited them either.

When it was time for dinner, which took place in a garden in Provence, in a scene of elaborately crafted beauty, curated by people who charge a lot for that sort of thing, they seated me next to a woman who held a high-ranking position in a company in the luxury industry, and as is often the case for those in such fields, she had been born wealthy. Something to do with British aristocracy. The woman, who seemed over six feet tall, had almost transparent skin and moved with the supreme confidence that must come from the knowledge that all the descendants of your descendants will also have real estate at their disposal. She was in her second marriage and had four children spread across Europe and the United States. Neither she, who lived in Paris, nor her husband, who directed all his companies from Vienna, lived under the same roof as any one of them. Each of the children, the two from the first marriage and the two from the second, was at that moment living in a different country. Some in boarding schools, others on their own, though they were still teenagers. On weekends, the family would meet up in different parts of the world. The arrangement, she told me, worked very well for them. They were all very content.

It struck me as strange, of course, because I am culturally programmed to see it as such. In the very middle-class family I grew up in, children were raised by their parents unless there was some catastrophe. In the last century, no one has had to leave their children behind and emigrate to another country to earn a living, but we also don't know of teenagers living alone in Manhattan penthouses.

My maternal grandmother did spend some time away from her parents; firstly because when she was born, they left her in the care of a wet nurse in a small village in the Basque Country while they were living in the provincial town of Vitoria, as was relatively common back then. And afterwards because they sent her to a boarding school run by Ursuline nuns, in the years leading up to the Spanish Civil War. Those two biographical details simultaneously terrified and engrossed me when I was young. I knew she got along better with her fake sister, the daughter of her former wet nurse, whom she called almost every evening, than with her biological ones, but the idea that her parents left her in a house in the country seemed exotic, and so did the boarding school. Pleased to have access to a local version of Enid Blyton's stories, I always asked her to tell me about her time there. The best and most grisly tale of all, an anecdote whose prosody she had perfected by repetition, was known as the mutton story. My sister and I had memorised it, but that didn't ever stop us from wanting to hear it just one more time.

Once, they were serving mutton for dinner at my grandmother's school. The meals always came on covered trays, brought to them by women in caps and white gloves. Or so she said. The part about the white gloves was very important and was included in the story without fail. What happened is, my grandmother hated mutton and didn't eat it. After a while, without a word, the same servers, who might have been nuns of a lower rank – in some orders, there was a distinction between nuns with a dowry and poor nuns, who were made to do all the dirty work – took away her tray. The next morning, when she went down to breakfast, the rest of the girls had milk and sweet buns. Not her – for her, they had brought out the reheated meat. Once again on a covered tray, which I imagined like the ones I had seen in comics, theatrical, convex, and very shiny. Once again, wearing those gloves. My grandmother still wouldn't eat it, stubborn in her hunger strike. Her stomach was growling, but she held her stance. She got through her morning classes as best she could, and at the next meal, which was lunch, of course the mutton appeared again. I don't remember at which point my grandmother gave in and ate it, if it was the third time or the fourth. The fact is, the ending was anticlimactic, and I didn't like it as much as the central drama.

When I listened to that story in her sitting room, which was governed by *horror vacui* and saturated with fabrics, cushions, porcelains, figurines, and silver frames, in a building with central heating where the temperature never fell below thirty degrees Celsius, the idea that they made her eat reheated meat for breakfast – I wasn't sure what mutton was then, but it sounded terrible – struck me as the epitome of cruelty. Just like living at a school without your parents. Someday I'll have to deal with my absurd fixation on boarding schools. Once, I retraumatised an author I was interviewing, an author who fascinated me, by

94

pointing out how appalling it was that he had been sent to a boarding school at age seven. 'Do you realise how young seven is?' I repeatedly asked the writer, who was unsettled by this line of inquiry, which had nothing to do with his novel. When my grandmother told me the mutton story, I wasn't equipped to understand that there are hardships much more severe than having to eat mutton. For example, having nothing at all to eat. The latter, of course, was much more common in Spain in the thirties, but I hadn't figured that out yet.

Something unusual happened that night when I met the aristocrat with four children scattered around the globe, the first night I spent away from my son. While I was silently judging that woman, who bore a greater resemblance to a blonde grey-hound than any other human on the planet, while I sentenced her for elitism and aloofness (snobbish, bad mother), with no possibility of appeal, other journalists at the dinner were doing the same thing to me.

'How many months is your son?' asked one woman, who had been sent by a women's magazine.

'He just turned three months,' I responded, my phone at the ready, prepared to show her a photo, or two hundred, of my trophy baby.

'What are you doing here?' she replied, not hiding her disgust. 'Why aren't you home with him?'

Unnatural, bad mother.

Just three months into the role, I wasn't yet used to saying 'my son', which still sounded false and foreign to me, but I had already learned very well that almost no one is exempt from dealing in those small collections of motherly guilt, doling out or receiving them, even when you'd least expect it.

Doris Lessing's Third Son

There's a scene in the novel *A Proper Marriage* in which the protagonist, Martha Quest, sits her three-year-old daughter on her knees, knowing, since she's on the verge of leaving her, that it will be the last time she does this, and says: 'You'll be perfectly free, Caroline. I'm setting you free.'

Lessing published the book in 1954, about a decade after living out a scene very like Martha Quest's, when she left her son, John, age three, and her daughter, Jean, one and a half, in the house she shared with her first husband and started a new life, hardly four streets over, in the same city, Salisbury (now Harare), in what was then Southern Rhodesia.

What happened with John and Jean was an abandonment in two parts. A few years after that first separation, the writer left again, but this time went further, to London. She took with her the manuscript of her first novel, *The Grass Is Singing*, and her third child, Peter, born from her second marriage, with activist Gottfried Lessing, a Jewish Marxist of Russian origin whom she had met in leftist circles in Salisbury.

She went to Europe, and her two elder children remained in Africa. That's one of the most well-known biographical facts about Doris Lessing. Even those with no particular interest in her as a person, nor in her books, know two things about her:

she won the Nobel Prize, and she abandoned her children. As in the case of Muriel Spark, with whom Doris Lessing shares many biographical details – what would have happened if these two women, so different but both trapped in unhappy marriages in the forties in Southern Rhodesia, had met? The speculation is irresistible – her troubled relationships with her children have become a part of her lore. Or maybe it only seems that way to me because it's a biographical point that fascinates the women of my generation in a very particular way. One of them, the British writer Lara Feigel, wrote an entire book stemming from it, entitled *Free Woman*. Among other things, Feigel, who idolises Lessing as an author, was grappling with her own difficulties understanding the decision. Whenever she mentioned the book she was writing (in 2018, not 1958), she was met with the same reaction: wasn't Doris Lessing a monster? Didn't she abandon her children? How could she have done that?

Faced with these questions from friends and acquaintances, Feigel readied several responses. First, she recited a list of bad fathers in art who had abandoned their children around the same time – Augustus John, Lucian Freud – then she threw out some historical context (the oppression of women, colonial asphyxiation, etc.). After that, she quoted Angela Carter in *The Sadeian Woman* – 'A free woman in an unfree society will be a monster' – and having recited that list, she had fulfilled her duty as a feminist writer. But even then, she found herself returning again and again to the same question, without needing anyone else to pose it: how could Doris Lessing have done such a thing? 'I was still trying to get my head round it all myself; still trying to work out how the love that I was convinced she'd felt for those children could have coincided with such ruthlessness. And I was confronting the worry that in defending her, I was somehow a monster as well.'

I have heard women who identify with so-called neoliberal feminism – which is more about valuing a superfemale than the community of ordinary women – who surely find the attacks on the feminist movement proffered by an elderly Lessing in the nineties transgressive and attractive, single the woman out precisely for that act of individual emancipation, considering her decision to leave home without her children the most important and radical thing the novelist did. More so than writing *The Golden Notebook* and three dozen other books. More so than strongly opposing apartheid and colonialism, more so than cultivating an independent and fiercely original mind for ninety-four years.

There are also ordinary feminists, less concerned about shattering glass rhetorically, who can't help but admire Doris Lessing's anti-sentimental boldness. Here's a woman capable of putting an ocean between herself and her domestic yoke in the forties, walking out on not just one husband but two to carve out her own destiny. And it goes without saying that leaving the children in Africa only heightens her courage. These two groups, which don't agree on much, both consider Lessing an icon of women's emancipation, someone who dared to do what so many others only dreamed of. She, at the end of her life, perceived the position she'd been placed in, and it made her uncomfortable. 'At least I'm ashamed of the lies I've told myself,' she once said on the matter.

The journalists who interviewed her understood that asking about her children was a dangerous feat they had to carry out if they dared, knowing that the author, who was cultivating a grouchy-old-woman persona, hated being made to speak on the subject. In 2001, for example, Barbara Ellen, of the *Guardian*, took a lateral approach. She asked why Lessing didn't talk more about the moment when she abandoned her children in her two volumes of memoirs. I do a lot of interviews, and I recognise Barbara Ellen's manoeuvre as a trick of the trade. It's like when you ask someone if it bothers them that so much weight is given to polemic X instead of having the nerve to come right out and ask about polemic X. We've all done it. Lessing replied:

> The truth is, people are angry because I didn't go on at length about how terrible I was to walk out on my children. What I should have done is written ten pages, saying: 'Oh, how could I have done such a thing, I'm so awful and wicked?' and then they would have loved it. On the contrary, I'm very proud of myself that I had the guts to do it. I've always said that if I hadn't left that life, if I hadn't escaped from the intolerable boredom of colonial circles, I'd have cracked up, become an alcoholic. And I'm glad that I had the bloody common sense to see that.

It's true that in her memoirs Lessing barely mentions 'the unforgivable', as she herself designated the act of her leaving John and Jean. The way she describes the moment of saying goodbye to her children in her memoir *Under My Skin*, the first volume, recalls what Martha Quest says to her daughter in *A Proper Marriage*. 'I was going to change this ugly world, they would live in a beautiful and perfect world where there would be no race, hatred, injustice, and so forth. . . . I was absolutely sincere.' Like Joni Mitchell and other women who took this step, Lessing never said she abandoned her children to write, nor to lay the foundation for a career that would win her the Nobel Prize. Her objectives were at once more and less ambitious than writing good books; her ambition was to create a beautiful world.

*

Doris Taylor, as she was named at birth, arrived in the world in what was then known as Persia, daughter of two semi-fortunate pawns of the British Empire: an ex-serviceman with a wooden leg and an ex-nurse with delusions of grandeur, who, like the Sparks and so many others, had come to understand that in the colonies, one could ascend a pair of rungs on the social ladder and access luxuries that were now cost-prohibitive in the mother country, like a house with domestic workers. Of course, there was a price to pay: Maude, Doris's mother, hated Rhodesia, the country her husband had dragged her to after Persia, with the vague promise that they would become land-owners. She arrived there in 1925 with a suitcase full of evening gowns, ready for a sparkling social life in ex-pat country clubs, and quickly realised the only thing she would do with those dresses was watch them turn little by little into muddy rags her children played with. She didn't get along well with her daughter, Doris, who left school (a boarding school for the children of colonial officials) at age fourteen. The mother's plans for her daughter to attend a school in England never materialised.

At nineteen, Doris married the man she deemed the least unappealing of her suitors at the Salisbury Sports Club. That was the only way for a woman to have an active sex life. For a teenager feverish with D. H. Lawrence novels, fond of stealthily reading a Dutch gynaecologist's sex manual, and moved, what's more, by the prime motive of not turning into her mother, Doris suspected her liberation would come via sex, and there weren't many ways for a young girl from a good family in Rhodesia to regularly attain it, besides marrying. Frank Wisdom was a civil servant ten years her senior. Both opposed the colour bar, the version of apartheid then in effect in Rhodesia, and read progressive magazines sent to them from England. They shared certain lax ideas about fidelity and wedlock. At that point, Doris already intended to write, and Frank vaguely supported her: What harm could it do for a woman to write a little?

Almost immediately after getting married, she became pregnant. In the summer of 1939, the world was on the verge of war, and the young couple had had no intention of procreating so quickly. Doris looked for a doctor who would give her an abortion, but the first one she found had been fined for operating drunk. The second told her she was already four and a half months pregnant and that it was now too late. All she could do was wait. At nineteen years old, Doris was going to become a mother, as the writer Julia Phillips says in her book *The Baby on the Fire Escape*, 'by those two fertility goddesses of the modern age: contraceptive failure and hope'.

As soon as baby John was born, the couple's tacit agreement was ruptured. They were no longer going to be a different kind of couple. As he saw it, they had already turned into the same thing as everyone else, a married couple with children in the colonies, and it took her longer to understand that. Their first months with the baby inspired some of Doris Lessing's most frequently cited lines. They aren't by a long shot her best, but they speak to that enthrallment with the writer as a woman who rejected motherhood, as if she had done nothing else in her life. They're phrases like those in *Under My Skin*: 'There is nothing more boring for an intelligent woman than to spend endless amounts of time with small children', and becoming a wife and mother is like climbing 'the Himalayas of tedium'.

Frank encouraged her to socialise with other young mothers. When they went to parties, the same boys who a few months before had been courting her now saw her as a venerable matriarch. She was realising that in the market of desire, nothing devalued a woman so much as becoming a mother did.

I was bored, I was rebellious, I hated the morning tea parties. I craved them, and hated myself for craving them. . . . Eighteen months ago, I – and all the other girls – had been competed for by every man in sight and now I had become invisible. I was treated as respectfully as if I had been fifty, in spite of my again slim body and my girl's face.

Moreover, John was not an easy baby. Restless and hyperactive, he could have inspired the boy Doris portrayed in *The Fifth Child*. Knowing all of that, how does one make sense of the fact that less than a year later, Doris was pregnant again? She answers the question herself in *A Proper Marriage*, in the voice of her alter ego, Martha Quest. 'You bore me to extinction, and that's the truth of it, and no doubt I bore you,' Martha says to her baby, Caroline, in the novel. But alongside that lethal tedium, that mountain range of weariness, Martha also feels an animal attraction to her child.

There were moods when a slow, warm, heavy longing came up, when the very sight of Caroline filled Martha with a deep physical satisfaction at her delightful little body and charming little face; and this was at the same time a desire to hold a small baby in her arms again. If she looked at one of her friends' babies in this mood, the craving was painful and insistent, and the adventure of being pregnant filled her entirely.

That's how, dragged along by maternal languor, Doris Lessing found herself returning to the Lady Chancellor Hospital of Salisbury one year after giving birth to her son, to give birth to her daughter, Jean. Shortly after the child was born, she and Frank went on a month-long holiday to Cape Town, leaving the children in the care of their neighbours. When she returned, she felt rejected by her daughter. Their relationship was always different from the one she had with John. Jean had a sweeter and more affectionate disposition generally, but Doris, who was already feeling an urgency to flee the domestic prison she had created, was attempting something impossible: she was avoiding becoming too attached to her own daughter. She describes this in her memoir: 'I was protecting myself, because I knew I was going to leave. Yet I did not know it, could not say, I am going to commit the unforgivable and leave two small children.'

She did it. In 1943, at age twenty-one, Doris Lessing left home, and left her two children there, both still basically babies.

The not-yet-writer found work as a typist in a law office and leased a small flat. Her main objective when she awoke each morning was to do something that justified having abandoned her children. She found the courage she was seeking in the small faction of communists in Rhodesia. She went to meetings, printed posters. And she fought with Frank to let her see the children. That entire first year, he forbade it. Doris's ex-husband, humiliated, remarried after just a few months, and his new wife began to play the role of mother for John and Jean.

Those intermediary years, when Lessing lived in Rhodesia as a separated woman, were especially tumultuous. The people she associated with shared her political outrage. She fell in love with successive English soldiers who were in Rhodesia training to fly planes for the Royal Armed Forces. She met the man who would become her second husband, the German communist Gottfried Lessing, whom she married in 1943 out of convenience: her British passport protected him. It was he who gave her the last name by which she is known. Their love was not the obvious kind. Shortly after leaving Frank and the children, Doris fell ill and had fevers that made her delirious. It was Gottfried who took care of her, bringing her ice cream and pastries. Neither the sex nor the cohabitation were especially pleasurable, but they maintained a certain polyamorous flexibility. Around that time, Doris also had a relationship with John Whitehorn, an RAF pilot.

If she were in love with at least one other man and already had two children she'd left behind, why did she have a third child? All Doris Lessing's biographers have asked the same question and have been met, in her letters and books, with contradictory responses. She writes to Whitehorn that she is going to have a son with the wrong man but is happy even so, because she misses John and Jean very much and feels lost without them. She tells another military friend, Coll McDonald, with whom she had a more candid relationship, not tinged with mutual attraction, that the pregnancy was the result of a disastrous experiment with a new contraceptive method, that Gottfried is delighted with the idea and she is not, but she'll pretend to be anyway. In her memoir, Lessing says she had her third child with Gottfried when they already knew that they were going to divorce, that it was the right moment, since they wouldn't have the chance later. That's the version a jury would be least likely to buy. She was only twenty-six, she had years of fertility ahead of her. Regardless, she went through with that third pregnancy. She was convinced the child would be a girl, whom she would name Catherine. That's how she referred to her constantly in her correspondence, with the name she had already picked out. It wasn't a bad pregnancy. In one of her letters to Coll McDonald, she compared the feeling of carrying a child to that of catching a bird in your hand. 'I believe women are always supposed not to like it, but I do. Primitive again. Sorry.'

The baby wasn't a Catherine, he was a Peter. Doris Lessing's third child was born in 1946, and in a situation that was far from ideal, she poured into him all the love she had been forced to keep from the others, whom she had scarcely been allowed to visit. 'My baby, if you are interested, is entirely admirable,' she told her lover John Whitehorn. She was surprised to feel 'suffused with the appropriate maternal feelings'. There were still Himalayas of tedium, surely, but in her writing she only leaves proof of an unambiguous maternal passion for her third child, the only one who, three years later, she took with her to England.

In 1949, Lessing arrived in London with a child, a manuscript, and two divorces behind her. If her life were a good miniseries, ready for the BBC or streaming, it would doubtless start up at this point. With all the vertigo and promise an indomitable woman might feel arriving in England from Africa, ready to tailor a life to her boldness.

Her thirties, which she describes in the second volume of her memoirs, *Walking in the Shade*, were defined by constant transit. New lovers, new novels, new causes to embrace, and several moves. Amid all that change, there was only one constant: Peter. Mother and son had an almost asphyxiating relationship. The thought of losing him caused her great distress. The boy carried the burden of being the only child present, a child who had to be worth three.

While Doris lives and writes, the boy is always on top of her, or next to her, or close by. The only exception was the rare holiday, during which she would leave him with an Austrian family she knew, who had a house in the countryside, in Kent, and then she could use the time to move forward her current project. She was always diligent with her dispatches. In that first decade in London, while making ends meet as a single mother, she managed to finish five novels, two story collections, one volume of her memoirs, and several plays.

Lessing was never able to recover John or Jean, whom she saw on their brief visits to London as teenagers. What she did do was open her home to many other boys and girls, whom she called her waifs and strays. From the sixties onwards, she adopted the role of universal mother for a series of teenagers who, with the city breeding sex and counterculture, had no way of relating to their own parents. The author fictionalised this experience in one of her later novels, *The Sweetest Dream*, published in 2001, when she was already over eighty, in which a forty-something woman named Frances adopts a band of neurotic teenage flowerchildren.

In the prologue of the book, Lessing does something unusual, and it seems a bit out of place there. She explains that she will not publish the third part of her autobiography as anticipated, because there are people in it whom she does not wish to expose. Her strays were heading towards middle age, and she didn't want to embarrass them.

That literary demureness is understandable, even laudable, but in fact, it was already too late. In London literary circles, it was perfectly well known that the most famous not-quite-daughter of Doris Lessing was the writer Jenny Diski, and some years later, anyone who wanted to would be able to read about the construction and terms of their very complex relationship.

By 1962, thirteen years after fleeing Africa with just one of her three children, the writer had become disillusioned with communism like so many of her generation's intellectuals, an experience she novelised in *The Golden Notebook*. Except in her case, that rupture was not only an intellectual exercise, of confronting the crimes of Stalinism, the tanks of Budapest, and more, but also a quite intimate one. 'I was married to a 100 per cent communist and, believe me, that cured you fast!' she joked in a 2001 interview in the *Guardian*.

Gottfried, Peter's father, never gave her any money for the boy's upkeep, because he had more important things to do, like the proletariat revolution. This behaviour was very typical among leftist males, who could see oppression in a factory in Hamburg or Detroit, but not in the kitchens of their own homes. As she distanced herself from the Marxist utopia, Doris became interested in Sufism, which emphasises personal growth and an acceptance of what life offers, especially the difficult or disagreeable, which is seen as motivation for improvement.

Who knows if it was that new philosophy and a chance to put it to the test, pure generosity, or the prospect of narrative intrigue – with novelists, you can never discount the hypothesis that they complicate their own lives to enrich their plots – but Lessing paid special attention to a letter from her son Peter, in which he wrote about a classmate, a girl of fifteen, the daughter of a criminal father and an unstable mother with self-destructive, melodramatic tendencies. In her relatively few years of life, the girl had already been expelled from several high schools, spent a period in a psychiatric ward, and lived in a kind of guest house while working at a shoe shop. The teenager, a true 'stray', was moored for a period at St Christopher's, the progressive high school Peter attended, because the institution accepted some difficult cases each year, as a charitable or social justice measure. 'Mother' – the letter began, very formal for a teenager – 'she is quite intelligent and it may be worth your while to help her.'

Without ever having met her, the author wrote her own letter to the girl, who at that time was still known as Jennifer Simmonds, and invited her to come and live in her home in

Mornington Crescent. If she didn't, thought Doris, the girl could end up pregnant and in a horrible marriage, or pregnant and dead, or pregnant, addicted to drugs, and dead. 'She considered that "pregnant" and "married" were alternate terms for "death",' the adopted girl wrote years later, once she was going by Jenny Diski and was a respected writer known for her mastery of sarcasm.

Lessing and Diski upheld a kind of literary nonaggression pact: I won't write about you, and you won't write about me. The elder of the two didn't respect it much: she used Diski as a model for several characters in her novels, and even informed her of the fact. 'This one is you,' she would say. As if that were necessary.

In 2013, the Nobel laureate passed away, and a few months later, Diski was diagnosed with terminal cancer. She recounted in an article that the moment she left the office of the doctor who had given her the worst news of her life, she knew the time had come to write about the woman whom she had never had a name for. Mother? No, she already had one, although she had cut off all contact with her in her youth. For years, Diski explains, she tried out various options. 'Benefactor', like in a Victorian novel. 'The woman I live with', practical but too ambiguous. 'Auntie Doris' made them both laugh. The project of writing about Doris Lessing gave her drive in her last months of life.

Diski titled the book in which she discusses her cancer and her complex relationship with Lessing *In Gratitude*, because she wanted to make clear from the first page that she was grateful for all that woman – once a complete stranger – had done for her. Giving her a home, allowing her to be a child again when the system had already shunted her to the least enviable zone of adulthood, teaching her by example that being a writer was a viable option. But somehow the title seems like a bandage for wounds that come later, because the book paints a ruthless portrait of Auntie Doris.

When Jenny became Lessing's protégée, there were consequences for everyone in the family, starting with Peter, the chosen child and the person responsible, in part, for that rare arrangement, the reconstituted family comprised of a divorced woman, her son, and a live-in teenager who wasn't even an orphan. Peter and Jenny had been schoolmates but not friends, and when they became de facto siblings, they found themselves in an unusual situation. Everything in Peter's life, in fact, was unusual.

At the end of his time at college, he failed all his exams, shut himself up in his mother's house, and barely ever came out again. He never had a job, nor a romantic or sexual partner. He suffered an intermittent depression for the rest of his life, as well as severe diabetes and heart problems. 'Peter's existence was the saddest and emptiest I can imagine,' wrote Diski, who also said the man, her not-quite-brother, was all his life a 'monstrous baby'. He died at age sixty-six, a few months before his mother, and Diski, distressed, spoke about how difficult it was to prepare his eulogy. What do you say of a man whose life ended when he was nineteen? The poems read were for children, by A. A. Milne, the author of *Winnie the Pooh*; the songs played were the ones he liked in high school. Beyond that, fifty years of blank life, spent as an appendage of his mother.

Peter and Doris grew old together, fighting and laughing at the same time, like those couples who learn over decades to tolerate each other's quirks. She never stopped taking care of him – there was never that role reversal wherein children must begin taking care of their parents.

Apparently, Peter once told a friend that the worst thing that could happen to him would be for Jenny to become a successful writer, which of course is precisely what did happen. The false daughter, the one he himself had brought into their home, had become the heir to the mother's gifts, and he was left with nothing. Lessing arrived at a similar conclusion and told several reporters that Jenny had been like the cuckoo in the nest. Cuckoo mothers put their offspring in other nests, and those offspring occupy the space of the legitimate chicks, often driving them out. Diski herself admits that she became a cuckoo, inadvertently. 'I was not a gift from Peter to his mother, but a curse. . . . I was a gesture, a question, a conversation he wasn't able to start with Doris. Perhaps, without mentioning the children back in Africa, he had tried to rebalance the family.'

Did Peter and Doris welcome Jenny in to replace the abandoned children? It seems like the conclusion a pop psychologist would draw – too clumsy, too easy. The family almost never explained it in that oversimplified way. We think we're above these kinds of explanations, and nevertheless, we formulate them all the time. When a child dies, for example, and the parents are still able to conceive, they're expected to do so as quickly as possible. One of my childhood friends was born a substitute daughter. Her parents had her one year after the sister she never knew died. The new daughter – my friend – and her ghost sister were identical.

In the same way, when a pregnancy doesn't fulfil its promise, when there's a miscarriage, everyone around the mother or the couple holds its breath until that woman is pregnant again. And then there's a tendency to believe that equilibrium has been restored, that everything is fixed, besides a residual grief. The idea that one child might substitute for another seems barbaric framed in the abstract, but it is also fully installed at our most basic subconscious level.

In her book, Diski also asks the fundamental question, the

same one Lara Feigel asked, and the one I'm asking here: how could Lessing have left her older children in Rhodesia? In fact, Diski writes that of all of Doris's 1949 journey, recounted one thousand times in the author's biographies, small child and suitcase containing the manuscript of her first book in hand (the suitcase is always mentioned, it's a very novelistic detail), what she's most interested in are the two children who stayed behind.

I grasp at that to feel justified. If Jenny Diski, who had lived more lives by fifteen than some people have by fifty, who published the best book about the sixties – titled, succinctly, *The Sixties* – who debuted with a novel about a sadomasochistic affair and was capable of incorporating anything into her writing, whether that was orangutans, the Old Testament, or her own cancer, with perfect pitch and not a trace of sentimentality (us women are always self-monitoring for signs of sentimentality and crow's feet), had also become stuck on that fact, then maybe I, too, could be obsessed with Lessing's children without having to call myself puritanical, unsophisticated, closed-minded, an obtuse reader.

> I am a feminist and a mother. I applaud the escape to freedom of a woman living her own life at such a time and in such a place, and her determination to fulfil her passion, to experience the power of her need to write. . . . I get the need to flee, but no matter how I try to put myself in her place, I am perplexed by her emotional ability actually to do it. I'm struck most of all by her finding a way to justify taking the one child and leaving the others.

Just like the biographers who have tried to rescue Doris Lessing from that most undesirable place, the swamp where bad mothers go, Diski concludes that the writer did it in part as a matter of pragmatism. It would have been absolutely impossible for her to survive with three small children, alone, in London – it was already almost a miracle that she was able to do so with one – and on the other hand, she knew the older children were well cared for by their father's family, while Peter's father had never made time to take care of him. In fact, as an estranged parent, he was irresponsible, negligent.

Doris Lessing was able to patch up her relationship with her older children, especially Jean, who had always had a more even temperament. The daughter went to London to visit her mother, who was by then already a famous writer, several times as a teenager. Diski writes in her memoir that they often saddled her with walking the girl around the city, that she was shy and had been raised with outdated values, that she would try on clothes she could never have worn in Rhodesia and page through books that wouldn't have made it through customs. John, who worked as a coffee farmer, died young, in 1992, of a heart attack. Jean, who took the last name Cowen as an adult, was the person who travelled to Stockholm to collect her mother's Nobel in 2007, since at that point, Doris was too old for a week of pomp and circumstance.

Prior to her death, the author established in her will that she would leave both Jean and Jenny the same sum, one hundred thousand pounds each, out of a fortune of some three million. '[Her will] does not reflect her great generosity towards many people, including myself, during her lifetime,' Jean said to the press in an elegant periphrasis. The most controversial aspect of the document was Lessing's decision to keep her diaries sealed. She made clear that they should remain so while Jean and Jenny were alive and that only her designated biographer (who ended up withdrawing from the project due to old age) would have access to her writings.

'I had never heard of anyone making sure they got the last word so effectively. So I thought I would get my own last word in before I pop off,' Diski explained in an interview.

Over a decade after her death, the authorised biography, which is now in the hands of writer Patrick French, has yet to be published, so we don't know what those diaries say about her children, biological or fostered. But we can read what she wrote in her novels about the experience of having them. In addition to being the 'epicist of the female experience', as described by the Swedish Academy when they gave her the Nobel – it would be nice to know what she thought about their use of the word 'female' – Lessing could be called the fabulist of maternal ambivalence.

The child psychologist Donald Winnicott outlined the concept in his most well-known article, 'Hate in the Counter-Transference', published in 1949. In a theory that ran contrary to the spirit of the time, the English paediatrician and psycho-analyst normalised and excused mothers who didn't constantly adore their children, even suggesting that those periods of maternal hatred are useful for a baby, who learns through them to tolerate the loss and frustration that will accompany him throughout life. 'Let me give some reasons why a mother hates her baby,' wrote Winnicott. 'The baby is ruthless, treats her as scum, an unpaid servant, a slave . . . He is suspicious, refuses her good food, and makes her doubt herself.'

The women in Lessing's novels themselves embody if not hate in the countertransference, then certainly maternal ambi-valence. They sacrifice themselves for their children and end up frustrated by that so rarely gratifying project. Often, those children turn into the principal source of their miseries, and the family home, a place where horrors are staged. Just over a year after publishing the work that established her as a writer,

The Golden Notebook, Doris Lessing released a story entitled 'To Room 19'. The whole thing is dotted with aphorisms on motherhood, as if she were reciting them to herself, or whispering them to the readers she'd won with her famous feminist novel. 'Children can't be a centre of life and a reason for being,' she writes. And also: 'They can't be a wellspring to live from.' She says the protagonist, Susan, must pay a high price for 'a gardened house' and a happy marriage.

This Susan marries late (which at that time meant maybe around twenty-eight) 'to general rejoicing', says the narrator, to Matthew, a solid, stable type – the word 'sensible' appears as many as seven times in the story in reference to the Rawling couple and what they represent – gives birth to four children one right after the other, and slides into mental illness to the point that she feels her only option is suicide. In her gradual transformation into an 'unreasonable' person, Susan senses that she has disappeared, that her authentic 'I' is 'in abeyance, as if she were in cold storage', while she performs the functions that are expected of a young wife and mother. This void that she detects is not only a vague unease, but manifests itself in distinct Mephistophelian figures that live inside Susan's aching mind. An 'enemy', a 'demon', a strange creature, 'a gingery, energetic man' whom the woman believes she sees in the garden. She goes as far as inventing a lover to justify her changed mental state to Matthew, because telling him 'what do you want, I'm a middle-class mother' seems like an implausible explanation.

That was the message Lessing wanted to telegraph to women in the sixties. *Achtung*, danger. Perhaps no other novel captures the terror that may result from the daring act of reproducing like *The Fifth Child*, which arrived long after 'To Room 19', in 1988, and has since held a unique place in many personal libraries. It is a novel both beloved and detested, sometimes simultaneously, a nightmare about motherhood that should never be gifted to pregnant women, unless you're a little sick.

The pair who serve as protagonists, as golden and shining as the couple in 'To Room 19', is made up of Harriet and David Lovatt, two shy and timid beings who seem made for each other. When they marry shortly after meeting, they buy a house that's too large for the two of them because they plan to populate it, as if it were a kind of abandoned region. They undertake this task diligently and gradually fill it with children. One, two, three, four, just like that, up until five, who the mother can already tell will be quite different.

That pregnancy is harrowing from the outset. The creature doesn't just kick, he doubles the mother over as he thrashes inside her womb. Harriet feels like hooves are scratching her inside flesh and imagines that she will give birth to a cross between two animals, a Great Dane and a little spaniel, or a tiger and a goat. When the child, whom they name Ben, is finally born, he is not far off from that mutant fauna: the baby is an ugly incubus, violent and malicious, who seeks to tear apart the entire family. He attacks his siblings, angelic creatures. He drives away the aunts and uncles and grandparents who used to flock to their welcoming home. Lessing, with twisted assiduousness, goes on adding increasingly cruel adjectives to her portrait of Ben, who is born muscled and long and roars like an animal and bites his mother's nipples.

Harriet also makes an attempt to abandon her monster child. When he has stopped being a baby and turned into a little domestic terrorist, she leaves him in an institution, a centre for children like him. But the mother feels remorse when she sees him in that nightmarish place, in a straitjacket, his yellow tongue hanging from his mouth like that of a beaten dog. So much so that she brings him home so he can continue destroying her life, until he joins a gang of criminals, leaving Harriet consumed, exhausted – an old woman at forty-five.

After separating from her older children, Doris Lessing did not experience anything like that goodbye again, not even in a symbolic sense. Her third child, Peter, never built himself an adult life, never removed his mother to that peripheral place children create for their parents as they grow. Jenny Diski recounts that Lessing became furious when she suggested that perhaps she should put her son-appendage in a flat, to foster his autonomy, just as small children are now encouraged to don their pyjamas alone, cut up their own hamburgers. There came a point when forcing Peter towards freedom was no longer realistic either. The third son took antipsychotic medication, suffered cardiac episodes, and needed someone constantly by his side.

When Peter died, Doris, who was then ninety-four, barely survived him by more than a month. Who knows if, alongside the grief, she felt that guilty relief parents of dependent children sometimes describe, having spent years divided between two conflicting fears: dying first themselves and leaving those children unprotected, or outliving their children and carrying on in incomparable pain. That seems like another, even crueller, form of maternal ambivalence.

Momfluencers and the Economy of Turbomotherhood

There's a place where each mother has roughly 4.3 children, where barefoot toddlers are a symptom not of parental negligence, but of status – who needs shoes? – where domestic chaos doesn't translate into mountains of dirty clothes and unwashed dishes in the kitchen sink. Here, any mess that might materialise does so among adorable landforms of blond wood and natural fibres. The place I'm referring to, obviously, is Instagram.

Social networks didn't invent the momfluencer. That vocation, which follows a very specific business model consisting of charging brands in exchange for including their products in one's personal family-life narrative, emerged initially in mum blogs at the beginning of the 2000s. But there, the culture revolved around sharing mistakes, not triumphs. Heather Armstrong, who launched the blog Dooce in 2001 and is considered one of the first women to monetise quotidian motherhood, and monetise it well – Dooce eventually came to earn forty thousand dollars a month in ad revenue – wrote about her depression and the challenges of caring for children while carrying on with one's own life. When Armstrong died by suicide in 2023, many of her readers felt the loss as something personal; they recalled how her posts brought them solace in the hazy days of early motherhood. Hers was a blog, so it was mostly made up of words. On Instagram, on the other hand, the currency is the image, and the design of the app itself promotes a winner's aesthetic in the subsection of momfluencers. They engage in a performative style of parenting that takes the concept of 'intensive mothering', developed by sociologist Sharon Hays in 1998, to its fullest extent. Hays defined the term in five points: an approach to mothering that is 'child-centred, expert-guided, emotionally absorbing, labour-intensive, and financially expensive'. Nowhere is this approach more visible than on a momfluencer's Instagram account, whether she's a fundamentalist Christian from the Midwest, a charismatic woman from the north of Spain with eight children, or an Australian who combines parenting with surfing.

I've spent more years than I can admit following a woman who lives in a small coastal town in California, with her partner and four children. In her home, which the husband has renovated with his own hands, everything is white or biscuit-coloured. When that husband, who always wears a three-day beard and strategically distressed jeans, finishes sanding the kitchen island, for example, or has just installed a shower on the patio – the house is in a constant state of improvement, these people are tireless when it comes to optimising their lives – he sits on the porch to play guitar, invariably accompanied by a harmonica which one of the children plays. During the summertime, although in reality they live in a tasteful summer year-round, a summer without sweat, a summer of linen and cotton, the children pull the little restored ice-cream cart out of the garage, with its umbrella that is neither orange nor parrot-green, but ochre, vintage, and adequately sun-faded. We've already established the chromatic discipline as quite important in this family. With what they make off the ice-cream cart, the kids can buy new guitars and skateboards, never electronics. The entire universe of this mother of four is curated like an art gallery, and the values she espouses are those of the analogue and the artisanal. An iPad has never snuck into a single frame of her stories.

This particular momfluencer lets herself take a more detached, meta tone when it comes to her own status. You can tell she really suffers when she has to make a paid post with the tag #ad, disclosing sponsorship as United States law has required since 2018, and she likes to occasionally dedicate a caption to how strange it is to think that this is how she's making her living, or spend a paragraph reflecting on the drift of the influencer economy. Those kinds of posts, which show something like self-doubt, usually feature the momfluencers on their own, without their children, assuring you their lives aren't quite how they look in the photos, feigning a certain disbelief over how they earn their daily bread.

The aesthetic of the Californian momfluencer, whose day-to-day I know more about than that of most of my friends, is reserved for a faction of public mothers oriented towards the college-educated middle class, and its totems come in the form of natural wood, wildflowers, and chequered tablecloths. The most successful representative of this subgroup is a woman named Courtney Adamo, an American based in Byron Bay (Australia), who presides over a small band of women in the area who self-define as murfers, a contraction of 'mum' and 'surfers'. The murfers make their own soap, which actually isn't that big a deal. I know of one Spanish momfluencer who makes artisanal crayons for her kids with leaves and flowers from her garden.

Something else the murfers do is have more than three children and fewer than seven. Adamo and her best friend, yoga instructor and entrepreneur Aimee Winchester, have five each, all with first names that could as easily belong to a brand of oat milk or a rabbit in a racist Disney movie from the forties.

Wilkie, Coco, Juniper, and Marlow frolic around Byron Bay and are almost always barefoot. The Californians too. A child without shoes, a child whose floor is so clean and safe that shoes are no longer essential, is a definitive status symbol.

Many of these women have launched their own products – bamboo bowls, vintage tricycles, handknitted baby sweaters for one hundred dollars each – but everyone knows that in general, they themselves are the real brand. They have a perfectly defined target audience, broad enough for them to earn plenty of money but also deliberately narrower than that of other momfluencers, who address a much larger group and are willing to sign contracts with brands that make plastic toys, disposable nappies, and sugary cereals, who take paid trips to Disney World at least once a year, and whose natural followers earn lower incomes and can't afford to be as concerned about getting it right with what they consume. The murfers and the professional mothers who make their own crayons would never pose with a pyramid of gifted nappies, nappies made of non-compostable cellulose and decorated with anthropomorphic animals.

Some members of the generalist group, like Lindsay Teague Moreno, a successful momfluencer who already has her own podcast and book, are even introducing what could be considered a reactionary antifeminist creed that situates itself between self-help and ultra-capitalism. They suggest all the problems of motherhood, and, by extension, of women, can be solved by way of self-discipline. Channelling the phrase some mothers use with their kids – you get what you get and you don't throw a fit – Teague Moreno writes in one of her posts that 'throwing a fit won't help'. But she's not speaking to fussy children, she's speaking to the women who demand the gender pay gap be closed.

In this group of mainstream momfluencers, the numbers are more serious, both in terms of followers and money. Here, the reigning users are those like Stacey Solomon, who describes herself in her Instagram bio as 'mummy to five amazing pickles', or Naomi Davis, otherwise known as @taza, whose performatively wholesome posts abruptly stopped around 2022, leaving her followers to wonder what was happening with her family.

Families with seven or eight children, like that of Verdeliss, an ex-waitress who lives in Pamplona and has a total of almost 1.5 million followers across her various platforms, are very common in this circuit. It's no coincidence that in the United States, a religion like Mormonism is vastly overrepresented here. The Mormons, explains journalist Jo Piazza in her podcast, already had experience making scrapbooks, albums that were like an analogue Instagram before the social network existed, and what's more, the current leader of the Seventh-Day Adventist Church encourages his followers to be hyperactive online because he considers it a very effective form of proselytising. So of course as soon as momfluencing took shape as a profession, Mormon mothers emerged as potential natural leaders. They arrived first and have imbued the entire sector with their homemade, rural aesthetic. The conservative momfluencers were also the Trojan horse that brought the Q-Anon conspiracy into the mainstream during the last years of Trump's presidential term, and many of them also signed on to the anti-vax agenda. The same women who posted photos of their babies in jack-o-lantern costumes were suddenly posting deranged videos about Hilary Clinton leading a paedophilia ring or Bill Gates implanting microchips. Other momfluencers, ones more likely to include linen and barefoot children, have also sometimes tended towards vaccine scepticism, but in their case, because they believed an immune system as effective as theirs and their offspring's required no chemical intervention.

In Spain, too, there's an important concomitance between Opus Dei, the ultra-right, and the world of social media influencers. The leader of the far-right party Vox, Santiago Abascal, is married to a lifestyle influencer, Lidia Bedman, who shares photos of her looks, recipes, and workouts with her followers. At the weddings of the most famous influencers, it's common to hear the Spanish national anthem, which is so partisan no one left-leaning would play it, as well as the military hymn. They've started to have children early, around twenty-five, with two decades of fertility still ahead of them, enough time for at least half a dozen.

Large families show up frequently in part due to the fact that the very algorithm that governs these networks rewards them (they offer more content possibilities), and in part because the new fertility cult very much resembles the old fertility cult.

For families who make their livelihoods in this way, every pregnancy is a priceless opportunity to refresh their brand. That's how they get high-quality content for their followers – the pregnancy announcement, the gender reveal, the ultrasound – each milestone is fodder for stories, captions, photos, and new sponsorship opportunities. The possibilities are endless, from a giveaway for organic cotton bandages to a deal with a manufacturer of child carrier backpacks.

Often, these women are accused of having children merely to feed the machine, as a pretext for narrative. Those who level this judgement have no doubt that the choice is immoral. Having a child for Instagram – could a person sink any lower? In fact, those women are adding children into their families the way it was done in premodern times, when extra hands were needed to work the field. Those children, Instagrammers since they were sperm, are the new labourers of the digital economy.

For obvious reasons – children cost much more money than they can generate – people no longer frequently take this approach in so-called developed economies. But the economic factor continues to be more decisive than any other in determining how many children one has, and when. Becoming pregnant with my second child was the most extravagant financial decision I'll ever make, more so than taking out a thirty-five-year mortgage at age twenty-nine, more so than giving up a permanent contract to return to freelancing, more so than studying journalism. I could have invested in a pyramid scheme, I could have started a poetry press, I could have bought a pony on credit, or a jet ski, and still, having a second child would remain the most unwise decision I've made in my life, taking income and expenses into account. Having that second baby obliged us to move into a new home, a more costly one, and pay three years of preschool tuition. My family's life became more expensive in every possible way.

I used to say I would have as many as three children if I could afford it, but I'm no longer sure I believe that. Would I really? After my second was born, one day as I sat at the dining room table, a current of clarity passed through me: I would never again have to be pregnant. The revelation jolted me with physical relief, like when you wake up from a nightmare. But that feeling didn't last long. As soon as child number two started to walk and talk, I turned back into that person who grabs other people's babies too insistently, who breathes in the scent of the napes of their necks, the one who routinely visits the new-born section at Zara, each time a little sadder, taking down little pairs of pants the size of bar napkins, looking at them, and returning them to their hangers as if I were in a bad movie about a woman who longs for a child.

I've figured out that it makes me more comfortable to hold capitalism responsible for my family planning. Thinking the reason I won't have more children is because I can't afford another two thousand euros a month for day camps every July, or several hundred euros a month for extracurricular activities, is easier than actually considering a complete lifestyle change. If I really wanted to have the third child my hormones sometimes clamour for not so subtly (what a cliché I am, that woman who stares too long at other people's babies at the pedestrian crossing), I could move to a less expensive place, throw my hat into the ring for a permanent position, do away with all frivolities, give up the bad habit of eating three times a day, sell organs on the black market. The options are infinite, really. In not exploring them, I save myself from having to ponder whether I have anything left to offer this hypothetical third child, aside from extreme fatigue and precarious mental health – the third child who would, for a time, wear shoes as small as a toy car, who would have eyelashes like awnings, and would wake up, like his siblings, with his hair a mess, smelling of Snuggle fabric softener and milk.

The process of going from zero children to one is so monumental and glamorous that it often takes up all the attention in our personal stories of motherhood. That's the one they write books and make movies about. But often the path from child one to child two, or from two to three, involves significantly more insomnia and self-interrogation. In *Scenes from a Marriage*, the Ingmar Bergman series, everything begins to collapse in the squarely bourgeois home of Johan, psychology professor, and Marianne, divorce lawyer, when she becomes pregnant with what could be their third child. In that house, there are already two little girls. 'It's your decision,' he tells her when he finds out about the pregnancy. And Marianne knows in that moment that either choice, having the baby or getting an abortion, will be bad, and in a concrete and painful way.

On the way from child one to child two, you also become

another person. When I had only one child, I often received this comment, almost always from younger women: you don't look like a mum. What they meant was, you're doing a good job, you're retaining a reasonable approximation of your market value, despite that defect devaluing you. 'At least you don't have a mum bod,' an old colleague let slip at one of the first parties I went to post-pregnancy, about three months after giving birth to my second son. He was drunk enough that he felt like he had the authority to act as an expert sent to perform a property damage assessment. In this case, the property was my body.

Now, almost no one congratulates me on hiding my condition as a mother well. I do look like a mother these days, a mother who can't be remedied, whose erotic, employment, and personal capital has clearly depreciated.

Annie Ernaux wrote in *A Woman's Story* about the decision to have a second child: 'I can no longer think of any way to change my life except by having a baby. I will never sink lower than that.' When I found the phrase, in the prologue of a tome entitled *Mother Reader: Essential Writings on Motherhood*, edited by Moyra Davey, I underlined it and marked it with a small arrow, but that was superfluous. I had already filed it in my hippocampus, and it would remain there forever. It's painful to be so transparent in the eyes of a French writer who doesn't know you.

In my environment (in one of my environments, at least), families with three children are relatively common, and I know I'm not the only one who, upon hearing the news of one of these third pregnancies, squints a bit – I have to do that to activate the distant part of my brain where mathematics lives – and makes a quick calculation, factoring in the probable salaries of the progenitors, their housing expenses (rent? mortgage? a house given to them by rich parents? the third option is surprisingly common) and the hypothetical additional income (a well-timed inheritance?) that has made the existence of this new human possible. The difficulty of maintaining work-life balance is often cited as one reason why families have become smaller. According to what I've observed informally, however, money carries more weight than any other factor when making a decision like this. There are many couples with extremely demanding jobs and punishing schedules who have three or four children for reasons that have nothing to do with religion. Simply put, they can afford to. I once saw this headline in the British press, always gifted when it comes to crafting an eye-catching phrase: the fourth child is the definitive status symbol.

In the sphere of momfluencing as well, the professional mothers' thousands of followers are invited to make a similar sort of calculation but bigger, every time a fourth, fifth, sixth, or seventh child joins the family. What new contracts will they sign? How many followers will this new baby get them on YouTube? What brands will join their list of sponsors? How much money is tucked under the arm of this new Instagrammable being?

In May 2020, month three of a global pandemic, millions who had lived peacefully up to that point without knowing who Myka Stauffer was learned her name. During that time, many people were shut up in their homes and in need of narrative stimulation, of stories that would activate their primary emotions – sadness, joy, anger – and, preferably, had nothing to do with the coronavirus. And in precisely that optimal moment, Myka Stauffer showed up in their feeds: an ex-nurse in Columbus, Ohio, thirty-something years old, devotee of the word of God and perfect curls.

When she became world famous, it had been a long time

since Myka had worked as a nurse. Her income, which was quite high, came from her Instagram account and the three YouTube accounts she managed with her husband, James. The Stauffers had over one million followers across their distinct channels: the family one, her personal one, and his, about cars and mechanics. The digital product they sold was directed towards the generalist segment of the momfluencer audience. They were white, blond, and Christian, after all, and big proponents of home-schooling. Their main monetisable value was how photogenic the children were, one she had brought to the marriage and three she and James had together. They were missing, perhaps, something that would differentiate them from other families that posted similar content every day. They needed a competitive advantage.

Myka had always been interested in adopting children, preferably from Africa, as she wrote in one post, and she had raised the subject with her husband several times in the videos they posted on The Stauffer Life, their main YouTube channel. James was always more hesitant. He wasn't quite seeing it. Finally, towards the end of 2016, James agreed, and the family posted a video to announce that their 'journey' was starting here.

In that key word, reality TV and self-help intersect. Everything is a *journey* now; a contestant's participation in a talent show, the cancellation and subsequent redemption of a celebrity, everything is a route towards personal growth or disaster, but disaster that you take advantage of, that teaches you something, or, if possible, gets you a book or entertainment deal. In this case, the *journey* to adoption would provide a new narrative line for the Stauffers to add to their offerings.

After spending some time getting informed on Facebook groups for adopting families, where their presence caused controversy (the families were confused by the very insistent blonde's questions), and also at agencies in the wild and dangerously unregulated US adoption market, the family decided that they were open to the possibility of providing a home for a child with serious health problems. Myka Stauffer said she spent months looking through agency photos, until she finally saw a little face that 'spoke to her'. Myka had found, in China and via a screen, her fifth child.

The Chinese orphanage informed them that the child could have a tumour or cyst and sent them a medical file, which they shared with their own US paediatrician. The doctor advised them that this could be a complicated adoption, but they continued forward 'without a doubt in [their] minds', as they explained in one of their videos.

They raised money from their followers so they could go and collect him in China (not much, according to later research – eight hundred dollars or so) and, always imaginative, came up with an ingenious and lucrative way of revealing the child's face. For five dollars, you could unlock part of a thousand-piece puzzle on Instagram, which, once complete, would introduce Huxley, the newest Stauffer child. Even before arriving at his future home, Huxley was already working for the family business.

When the time came, the couple and their four biological children travelled to China for what is known in some corners of Instagram and YouTube as 'Gotcha Day': the 'pick-up day', a popular name (also used for adoption of dogs) that refers to the day when adopters meet the adoptee. Adoption specialists and activists roundly reject the term for some two thousand different reasons. It turns minors into objects; reinforces the white-saviour concept, if the adoption is international and trans-racial; and goes against all the pedagogy surrounding the welcoming of the adoptee as an integration of equals.

That didn't matter to the Stauffers. 'Gotcha Day' is catchy

and it's a good SEO keyword, so they used it to title their video, which they dedicated to 'all the orphans around the world'. In the background, they added an upbeat Swedish pop song. In no time, it had five and a half million views, much more than their videos averaged.

The trip to China marked a before and after for the Stauffer family channel. They went on to have a much larger subscriber base and started posting new content every day, when before, they had only posted three videos a week at most. The public wanted more, much more, of that family with four white children, one Chinese adoptee, and young, athletic, charitable parents. Unlike that of the Australian momfluencers, the lifestyle of the Stauffers didn't seem threatening. They gave frozen fish sticks to their children, bought them shakes at McDonald's, and let them watch cartoons on their giant TVs. There was nothing to fear there. Their audience felt reassured, not judged, by their parenting choices.

Huxley began to show up in the videos, playing with his siblings, dancing, laughing. Most have now disappeared from the internet, but the family's digital footprint had grown so large that some are still easy to find. In one of them, you can watch the child learning to say *apple*. He stumbles on the word several times, and the mother repeats it in front of the camera. In the momfluencer sphere, it's common for one child in a family to generate much more traffic than the others. Usually the youngest, or the cutest. The metric functions the same way it did in eighties and nineties sitcoms, in which whole narratives were contrived simply to maintain a constant supply of children under the age of five. When the baby of the star family grew up, a replacement was quickly provided. It happened in *The Bill Cosby Show*, and in *Growing Pains*, when an awkward moustache showed up on the face of young Ben and they looked for another blond boy, this one with much more spark: Leo DiCaprio.

You can't access the data now, but it's clear that Huxley improved the Stauffers' numbers. They often chose him for thumbnails, the fixed images used to advertise YouTube videos, and they featured him in some of their special promotions. On one Instagram post paid for by the detergent Dreft, for example, Myka Stauffer comes out with a laundry basket (plastic, not wicker, because Myka is a general momfluencer, not the organic kind) and rubs noses with Huxley, an adorable picture of whole-some, and well-paid, motherhood.

The Stauffers have always denied using Huxley for monetary gain, and that all money made from his posts went towards his care. However, they took advantage of his presence to pivot towards adoption and special needs content and often talked about the challenges of raising him, always stressing that if this was the plan God had for them, all they could do was accept it with their biggest smiles. Several months into life with his new family, the child was diagnosed with level-three autism as well as attention deficit disorder. The parents said in one of their videos that they felt deceived by the Chinese adoption agency, who had assured them that the child had no serious health problems.

Although Myka continued exploiting that path, writing arti-cles about education, adoption, and special needs for various digital publications, Huxley started appearing less and less in their videos. 'He's in therapy,' they would say. Or 'He goes to bed earlier.' That way, they said in one video, they could spend some quality time with their other children, the biological ones. That small detail was enough to arouse suspicion for some of their followers, who up until then had been very docile, satisfied with the free content the Stauffer channels provided. Some of them attempted to stage a rebellion and started to ask what was going on with Huxley. On 3 May 2020, someone used an anonymous account to post: 'Myka, we are very worried about your son . . . Deleting IG comments and avoiding questions inquiring about Huxley and his whereabouts is extremely suspicious and worrying. We won't stop until we have #justiceforhuxley.' A hashtag was born.

Less than a month later, the Stauffers offered the explanation their followers had demanded. Isn't that how it works? Doesn't watching all those YouTube commercials before you could 'skip ad' give you the right to know the whole truth? James and Myka put themselves in front of the camera, dressed in white, him looking calm, her with a face that showed she had been crying, as is expected of a remorseful mother, a mother who no one would suspect of sedating her daughter in a resort in Portugal, or killing her baby and blaming it on a dingo. The couple explained that they had 'rehomed' Huxley, in what would be his 'forever home'. The concept of the 'forever home', like 'Gotcha Day', is part of the new glossary of adoption.

In a note that remains on her Instagram, written with tortured syntax, Myka Stauffer confesses that she succumbed to naivete and arrogance in thinking she could handle Huxley's adoption. That they didn't make money off the child, that all their income from videos featuring him was, in the end, put towards his care, and that 'moms need a safe space to ask for help when they are struggling'.

I would have to bring together several linguistics and sociology departments in order to fully analyse the language in that video and that post. The neologism 'rehome', which is usually used in reference to pets, and the mention of the 'safe space', which originated in feminist and LGBTQ+ groups describing spaces without cisgender, heterosexual men, used in the context of a

Christian Instagrammer's post, seems to exemplify a troublesome postmodern irony.

The only six comments left are filled with hearts and support, doubtless because the thousands made up of insults and threats were deleted.

As one might expect, when the Stauffers were cancelled, Myka was the target of about fifteen times more rage from their followers, and anyone else who found out about the story, than James. At the time of writing, he's still running his YouTube channel about cars, Stauffer Garage, which has more than one million subscribers. She, on the other hand, just keeps an inactive Instagram in her name, but it still has more than 152 thousand followers, just in case she one day decides to return to public life. So far, she has yet to find the path – a new *journey* – towards reputational rehabilitation. She stays away from the social networks. All the brands that sponsored her disappeared in a flash, many making sure to release a statement beforehand, explaining that they would no longer be supporting the woman who got rid of her adopted son with special needs.

The timing of the Stauffer incident couldn't have been worse. It exploded while Donald Trump was spending every day tweeting about the 'China virus' and the 'Wuhan virus', when there was a surge in attacks on people of Asian origin in the United States, and the exact same week that policeman Derek Chauvin murdered George Floyd by asphyxiation and the video of the event unleashed a wave of protests against racial injustice. In that climate, 'rehoming' a neurodiverse Asian child didn't exactly make you popular on the internet.

The logic of the internet dictates that everything that happens must be followed by a reaction, which means that every reaction also generates a reaction. Although one might imagine it difficult to break the unanimity when it came to what happened with Huxley, the digital market of opinions rewards dissident voices, and a few valiant women also emerged (these matters are always settled among women), willing to write articles about their own failed adoptions or express an understanding of what brought the family to send Huxley back.

It is estimated that approximately one in every seventy adoptions ends with a child returned to the system, although scholarship sometimes also counts as failed adoptions those in which the adoptive parents retain custody but there is not a good relationship between them and the child, and at that point, it's almost impossible to determine how many of these stories end badly. The matter is especially opaque because, until recently, these experiences of adoption and abandonment were kept hidden in the corner of shame.

In a parallel universe, the Stauffer story might have been semi-secret, too, recounted in a low voice on sites like FosterClub or Adoption.org, where there are versions of accounts titled something like 'My failed adoption'. Reading them one after another is gut-wrenching. Even those in which it seems obvious that the parents never should have undertaken this *journey* and are equipped with selfish neo-colonial ideas end up being devastating. But those defeated parents aren't internet celebrities.

The Stauffer case, on the other hand, took place in front of the whole world. And Huxley was not just a child. He was also social media content. For a short time, without being consulted by anyone – child labourers never are – he toiled for likes. He advertised detergents. He struggled immensely to learn to speak English, with an iPhone camera in his face.

After the episode, Myka saw her career as a domestic influencer thwarted – although with over one hundred thousand sleeping followers, the temptation to return and *reinvent* herself must be huge – but the culture that produced her account and thousands of similar ones is still in peak health. Emily Hund, an affiliate of the University of Pennsylvania Center on Digital Culture and Society whose research focuses on the influencer industry, states that accounts related to motherhood and domesticity are responsible for 30 per cent of the total business, which is to say, they're allotted one third of the fifteen billion dollars she estimates the industry turns over each year.

In Spain, there are also several dozen professional mothers who can demand around one thousand euros from brands for each Instagram post, for featuring them among photos of their children and themselves. The market is huge, and anyone can choose to follow an authorised 'bad mum' who jokes about sometimes feeding her children frozen cordon bleus, a witchy mum who loves essential oils, or a Montessori mum. The range is limitless.

Somewhere in California, in a little surfing town where the sun is always pleasantly subdued, a woman is setting fairy lights out on the porch. There is a baby attached to her hip with an ochre-coloured wrap, and another one of her children is playing with a vintage film camera (little Dex is the artist of the family). I'll see it when I'm scrolling through Instagram on my phone instead of reading, or working, or playing with my own children, of which there are only two, not five, not seven. I'll look at her little fairy lights, but I won't give the image a heart.

Nora Helmer and Anna Karenina:
Stray Creatures

For a very brief period, the most famous abandoner of her children in modern literature stopped being one. The play *A Doll's House*, by Henrik Ibsen, arrived in Germany in 1880, barely a year out from its Copenhagen debut and already tinged with an aura of triumph and scandal. Henrik Ibsen's agent believed the original ending, in which Nora Helmer, an upper-class Norwegian woman, leaves her husband and three children to try and become 'a reasonable human being', would not be well received in Martin Luther's country. And the actress who had been chosen for the German production, Hedwig Niemann-Raabe, refused to act the final scene because she felt incapable of identifying with a woman who leaves her children. Probably, she was also worried about the potential effect on her reputation off stage.

So, between the two of them, they pressured the dramatist to write an alternate ending in which Nora's husband, Torvald, obliges her to go into the children's room once more before leaving. Ibsen accepted, knowing that if he didn't, any other German playwright might have interfered in his text – copyright laws were lax then – and preferring to do so himself. What is now known as the 'German ending' turned out like this:

NORA: . . . Where we could make a real marriage out of our lives together. Goodbye. [*Begins to go.*]

HELMER: Go then! [*Seizes her arm.*] But first you shall see your children for the last time!

NORA: Let me go! I will not see them! I cannot!

HELMER: [*Draws her over to the door, left.*] You shall see them. [*Opens the door and says softly*] Look, there they are asleep, peaceful and carefree. Tomorrow, when they wake up and call for their mother, they will be – motherless.

NORA: [*Trembling*] Motherless . . .!

HELMER: As you once were.

NORA: Motherless! [*Struggles with herself, lets her travelling bag fall, and says*] Oh, this is a sin against myself, but I cannot leave them. [*Half sinks down by the door.*]

HELMER: [*Joyfully, but softly*] Nora!

[*The curtain falls.*]

It turns out the agent and actress were wrong. This alternate ending, in which Nora reconsiders and stays at home for the well-being of her children, did not work for German audiences, and it was retired after a short while. Ibsen always rejected it and considered it a 'barbaric act of violence' that betrayed his original work.

It's well known that in *A Doll's House*, Nora leaves at the end of the third act, abandoning her husband and three children because she cannot tolerate continuing to play the role of the slightly unwell wife, a little crazy, but good deep down. She has seen the truth of things and no longer has the will to be someone's little squirrel, someone's lark, someone's songbird. All names her husband, Torvald, calls her throughout the play, names fit for a woman-child, someone who isn't quite capable.

Ibsen always maintained that he hadn't intended to write a feminist play. When they invited him to speak before the Danish Women's Society in 1898, he explained that he didn't typically write 'to further a social purpose', adding, 'I thank you for your good wishes, but I must decline the honour of being said to have worked for the Women's Rights Movement. I am not even very sure what Women's Rights really are.'

There is an ample academic branch very intent on divorcing Ibsen from feminism, which has devoted itself to defending precisely that idea: that *A Doll's House* is about a specific woman who wants to be a person, not about women as a whole demanding to be considered one half of humanity.

In the notes he made before writing the play, however, the author did make clear that he worried about what women could do after (or in addition to) becoming mothers. A mother in modern society, he wrote, is like 'certain insects who go away and die when [they] have done [their] duty in the propagation of the race'.

The work became the preferred topic of conversation among the Nordic middle class when it debuted. It is said that in some Scandinavian homes, where peace and absence of conflict are prized, that the play was explicitly referenced on dinner invitations: 'Conversation about *A Doll's House* is prohibited.' Because if the topic did come up, quarrels were guaranteed. Some political and ecclesiastical readings of the work denounced Ibsen for having written something not dangerous, but unrealistic, since women are noble and maternal, and no one would believe that a good woman from a solid family, who has never before shown any trace of malice, would be capable of abandoning her three children in such a way.

A theologian from Kristiania University College in Norway described *A Doll's House* as 'ugly and distressing'. The critic

M. W. Brun wrote in *Folkets Avis* that any real wife would 'throw herself into her husband's arms' at the end of the play. In that final act, Torvald forgives Nora for her mistakes – going into debt to take him to a southern climate so he can recover from an illness, hiding it from him – and assures her they have a bright future together. From now on, promises Torvald, he will be husband and father at the same time. His pardoning her makes him feel magnanimous, and he revels in it: 'There is something so indescribably sweet and satisfying, to a man, in the knowledge that he has forgiven his wife – forgiven her freely, and with all his heart. It seems as if that had made her, as it were, doubly his own: he has given her a new life, so to speak; and she has in a way become both wife and child to him. So you shall be for me after this, my little scared, helpless darling.'

Of course, an alternative reading existed from very early on as well. Which is to say, there were readers who did see the text as a guide for emancipation. In England, the fact that the translator, the first interpreter and foremost promoter of the work, was the feminist and labour pioneer Eleanor Marx, daughter of Karl, was key. That meant the play was already a politicised event, even before it had been performed in the country. In China, there was a powerful Ibsenist movement at the start of the twentieth century. The playwright Hu Shi adapted *A Doll's House* for a Chinese audience, and it is believed that many Chinese women, prompted by their readings of *A Doll's House*, abandoned their homes or refused to accept arranged marriages. It's not clear whether this actually happened or if it's one of those semitrue legends linked to literature, like the famous Werther effect, which suggested that a youth suicide epidemic ran through Europe after Goethe's *The Sorrows of Young Werther* was published in 1774.

More than one hundred and forty years after it debuted, *A Doll's House* cannot be separated from its feminist implications, despite some scholars' attempts. Apart from the most reactionary, today's viewers won't find it hard to detest Torvald Helmer, an emotional manipulator who, in the span of two pages, goes from calling his wife a hypocrite and a criminal – daughter of her father, another hedonist – to promising he will 'advise' and 'direct' her as if she were his daughter. Read in pop-psychology, twenty-first-century terms, Torvald is an especially noxious model of the 'toxic husband', and Nora is a newly empowered woman on her way to self-realisation.

On that point, everyone can more or less agree. In terms of the root moral question, however, things haven't progressed quite so much. Is Nora doing the right thing when she abandons her children? The writer A. S. Byatt, author of novels such as *Possession*, published an article entitled 'Blaming Nora' in the *Guardian* in 2009, in which she writes that each time she reads the play, she judges Nora with less compassion. 'Silly' is the word she uses to describe her; not 'bad', not 'imbecilic', which at least have more substance to them, just 'silly'. Not even after more than a hundred years of feminism has Nora broken free from the world of diminutives.

'Great tragedy asks us to care for flawed or even stupid people – Pentheus, Othello, Macbeth – but the glory of *A Doll's House* is that it asks us to care for a small-minded person, in the moment of her realisation of her own small-mindedness,' says Byatt, reproaching Nora for being unsympathetic, unable to see beyond her own domestic drama, laughable compared to so many other dramatic heroes. Byatt even expresses pity for Torvald: 'He, too, is a person of limited imagination. He too, I think, has a right to our sympathy, a man trapped in a doll's house.' She forgets to say, however, that the doll's house is in his name, that he has the key, and that when he leaves the place, he's allowed to function as an adult, unlike his wife.

Perhaps more interesting than A. S. Byatt's criticisms are the reports written by high school students around the world, many of whom are required to read *A Doll's House*. There are websites like SparkNotes, 123HelpMe, or GradeSaver, where you can access essays about all the works in the Western canon, which the laziest students copy and paste when it's time for them to turn in their own projects. Almost everything you find there are pretty pedestrian recitations of textbook arguments, but take a deep dive into the forums and you'll inevitably find some very pure and stimulating reflections. They're written by virgin readers facing monumental texts without any interference from academia.

These young readers do everything you supposedly shouldn't do when you're analysing a text. They read as Virginia Woolf said to, 'not by sitting on the bench among the judges but by standing in the dock with the criminal'. They project themselves onto the characters, they make moral judgements, take sides, they adore or detest them. What's more, when those students talk about books, they do so using a curious mixture of colloquialism, neologisms, and therapy-speak, the psychologist idiolect in which many of today's essays and articles are written. The result is irresistible.

For example, in one essay available for purchase on 123HelpMe – not even sharing texts for plagiarism is free now – a US student compares the maternal abilities of Nora, whom she considers 'naturally a good mother', with those of another literary outcast, Emma Bovary, 'a false mother'. She explains: 'Whenever she wants to love and show affection she does, but when she is too busy shopping or having affairs, she would ignore her or think bad [sic] about Berthe.' Rachel Cusk says the same thing, but more articulately, in *A Life's Work*: 'Motherhood for Emma Bovary is an alias, an identity she occasionally assumes in her career as an adulterer. She is the essence of the bad mother: the woman who persists in wanting to be the centre of attention.'

On the GradeSaver forum, one student contemplates whether Nora's final action is justifiable. And another responds that it is not. 'In my opinion, you should never, ever just walk out on your children. She had no intention of even taking them or seeing them!' she writes, scandalised. The student also acknowledges, with respect to Torvald, that 'dealing with a man that only loves you only sometimes can lead any [woman to go] insane', but even so, she concludes that Nora's flight is premature. And another reader warns: 'She needs to invest some energy in making sense of who she is as an individual or she will never be much else besides somebody's really little doll.' *You go girl,* these modern readers are saying to Nora. *You slay, queen.* But also: how could you even consider abandoning your children? Are you crazy?

These days, the savviest students, who know that everything must be analysed from an intersectional perspective, don't miss the fact that Nora is not the only mother in *A Doll's House* who winds up living separately from her children. Anne-Marie, the nanny, also lives in the Helmer house, caring for three children and having cared for Nora, too, when she was a little girl and orphaned by her mother. To do that, to enter into service, she had to leave behind her own daughter, whom she will never see again.

The principal interaction between Nora and Anne-Marie takes place in the second act, when the lady of the house is already weighing up the possibility of a future without her children if her problems don't resolve. 'Do you think they would forget their mother if she went away altogether?' she asks her nanny. 'Nurse, I want you to tell me something I have often wondered about – how could you have the heart to put your own child out among strangers?' Anne-Marie responds with a working-class pragmatism: 'I was obliged to, if I wanted to be little Nora's nurse.' Her boss goes a step further: 'I suppose your daughter has quite forgotten you.' 'No, indeed she hasn't,' the nanny says. Her daughter has written to her twice: when she was confirmed, and when she was married.

I hope a young playwright is moved to retell *A Doll's House* from Anne-Marie's point of view, doing with her what Jean Rhys did with Antoinette Cosway in *Wide Sargasso Sea*, rescuing the crazy woman in the attic in *Jane Eyre* and conjuring a classic text out of another.

At the time of this dialogue in the play, Nora is still just play-acting tragedy, daring to allow her thoughts (and words) to stray towards a possibility she trusts she won't need to action. And it's possible that Anne-Marie herself plays a role in her decision-making process. In the play, which is very short, often described as not having a single superfluous word, Nora does not take the time to explain to Torvald why she doesn't consider taking her children with her, but it's clear that a nanny won't fit into the uncertain life she faces once she leaves home, and that would be a defining loss for the three children. Leaving them at home with their father, social status intact, she ensures that she won't drag her children with her as she declasses.

All the dramatic abandoners of nineteenth-century literature share this concern. It's one thing to line up before the abyss themselves, and something else entirely to pull their offspring along.

It's just as clear to Anna Karenina, once she has seen that a romance with Vronsky is going to be inevitable, that in order to live that love story, she will have to sacrifice her son, Seryozha, because children, and very especially male children, belong to their fathers, and therefore to their fathers' castes. Bringing them along would require removing them from the system and breaking their futures. Things they understand to be a part of day-to-day life seem improbable in the social class they're entering. How would they pay the nannies? Where would they find tutors for the children?

Both Nora and Anna arrived in their authors' imaginations by way of two true stories very close to them. Ibsen was inspired by what happened to his friend, the Norwegian-Danish playwright Laura Kieler. Laura fell ill with tuberculosis and hoped to go south to recover; Nora's problems stemmed from forging her father's signature to take her husband to Italy for a rest cure. Laura Kieler also carried a debt, and when she couldn't pay it off, she forged a cheque. Her husband, a schoolteacher, found out, cut her off, and locked her up in a sanatorium. Later, they reconciled. Kieler's friendship with Ibsen, on the other hand, did not survive the premiere of *A Doll's House*. She couldn't forgive her old confidant for snatching away her story, transforming her into the universal symbol of the desperate woman. When one writer steals a story from another, the betrayal is double: they're also taking material.

For Tolstoy, the story of an adulterous woman was also very close to home. Before writing *Anna Karenina* – a project that he began as a means of putting off editing the novel he really wanted to publish, about Peter the Great – he had watched his sister Mariya (or Maria) divorce. Like Anna, Mariya left her husband in Russia, but she took her three children with her to live with her lover in Argel. There, also like Anna, she had another daughter, but when her new partner abandoned them, she was forced to return to Russia with her husband and leave that daughter behind. Despite his conservative and traditionalist beliefs around family, Tolstoy had advised Mariya to leave her husband in the first place, a decision he later regretted.

If *A Doll's House* is concise and compressed, *Anna Karenina* is torrential, tumultuous. In the eight hundred pages of Tolstoy's novel, Anna has time to exhibit the full range of emotions that a mother can hold for her children, including furious maternal ardour, disenchantment, wild nostalgia, and also a kind of mild conformity.

When the novel opens, Seryozha is eight years old. Anna, whom Tolstoy portrays as a being who oozes spontaneous passions, adores him, although she has learned to calibrate her affections. 'And her son, like her husband, aroused in Anna a feeling akin to disappointment. She had imagined him better than he was in reality. She had to let herself drop down to the reality to enjoy him as he really was,' the narrator tells us. Even so, Seryozha is the main reason Anna hesitates to leave her husband, Karenin, and flee with her lover, Vronsky. And when she finally decides to do just that, Anna imposes her separation from the child upon herself like a punishment. Karenin eventually offers her a divorce, which could ease things, but she refuses and goes to Italy as an adulterous, condemned woman. 'I have done wrong, and so I don't want happiness, I don't want a divorce, and shall suffer from my shame and the separation from my child,' she says.

Though she's committed to having a bad time, the truth is that at first, she doesn't miss the child much. Tolstoy makes Anna repeat again and again that she can't live without her son, but what we see her doing is quite the opposite, until there comes a moment when Anna admits this to herself: 'I thought, too, that I loved him, and used to be touched by my own tenderness. But I have lived without him, I gave him up for another love, and did not regret the exchange till that love was satisfied.'

Anna has another daughter with Vronsky, Annie, for whom she will never feel the love that fills her when she thinks about Seryozha. The boy, abandoned by his mother, grows up poisoned by his father's new confidante, the hateful Lidia Ivanova, who goes as far as telling him his mother has died and convinces his father to disregard the letters Anna sends begging to see her son.

Raised by only one of the warring sides, Seryozha wants nothing but to become a replica of his father, a righteous man, a serious servant of Mother Russia. Near the end, when Anna hurtles towards her tragedy and the boy is not called Seryozha anymore but Sergei, having outgrown adolescence, she lives in a state of exalted confusion, driven mad by her jealousy of Vronsky. She has lost all sense of time and reality, and when she sees some children playing in the street, she thinks of her son. In some way, Seryozha, for her, will always be eight years old. She hasn't realised that he is already almost a man, that she missed half of his childhood.

Anna is the only abandoning mother in *Anna Karenina*, but not the only mother who suffers. She represents the conflict, like Nora's, between selfish happiness and love for one's children. Dolly, her sister-in-law, feels at times overwhelmed raising her six children with an unfaithful husband, Oblonski, and stays loyal to Anna almost until the end, but Tolstoy uses her as a cautionary tool, like the children's book character who learns a lesson. Dolly is one of the few people who breaks the social boycott against Anna and visits her in the luxurious home she shares with Vronsky after separating from Karenin. When she does, she is scandalised to learn that Anna doesn't want to have any more children with her lover, preferring to maintain her attractiveness for a bit longer. She is afraid of going bad, afraid for Vronsky to see her as a mother. Dolly is also appalled that Anna lives apart from her elder son. After that visit, she returns home relieved to have kept her six children close, and to remain inscribed inside the social order.

The academic Gary Saul Morson has written that Dolly is, for her author, the real heroine of *Anna Karenina*. She represents the ordinary woman, one with some common sense, a firmly rooted Russian compared to narcissistic, romantic Anna. The responsibility of embodying Leo Tolstoy's conventional ideas about family falls on Dolly.

There's one more mother in the tryptic the novel creates, Kitty, Dolly's sister, whom the author considers fit for all feminine virtues: marriage (she marries for love, not out of self-interest or sexual fervour), caretaking (she looks after her dying brother-in-law), and motherhood. Kitty only has one son over the course of the whole novel, and she is happy with him, but even so, the princess, introduced early on as a marriageable beauty, struggles somewhat to adapt to her new reality. Tolstoy grants her a minute degree of maternal ambivalence, as if to acknowledge the difficulty of the job.

Although the author's mother died when he was eighteen months old, he had many mothers nearby to inform him on that matter, starting with Sofia, his wife, who gave birth to thirteen children. When he was writing *Anna Karenina*, they were already on their ninth. Sofia was a prolific diarist – Doris Lessing was dazzled by her writings – and the couple had the habit of reading each other's diaries, something they started doing shortly after they married when Leo made Sofia read the full story of his childhood, including descriptions of moral and sexual turmoil that left her shocked. So it's quite likely that Tolstoy had his wife's writings in mind when he imagined these young mothers, their doubts and their sorrows. Anna, Dolly, and Kitty, each with her own uncertainty in tow.

When she had already given birth to four children, Sofia wrote in her diary, 'With each new child one sacrifices a little more of one's life and accepts an even heavier burden of anxieties and illnesses.' And also:

> I was wondering today why there were no women writers, artists, or composers of genius. It's because all the passion and abilities of an energetic woman are consumed by her family, love, her husband – and especially her children. Her other abilities are not developed, they remain embryonic and atrophy. When she has finished bearing and educating her children her artistic needs awaken, but by then it's too late, and it's impossible to develop anything.

Several times over the course of her childbearing years, Leo Tolstoy's wife expressed a desire to stop having children, but he always refused. For him, the essence of marriage was multiplication, and it was to continue until nature put an end to the family's reproductive career. There's a lot of Sofia in Dolly, and a lot of Mariya in Anna.

Almost the entire social scaffolding that supports both *A Doll's House* and *Anna Karenina* and makes their plots believable has now been dismantled. Anyone can divorce if they can afford it. Shared custody exists. Women are not, in name, the property of their husbands or fathers. It's not even necessary to pair off, nor reproduce the heterosexual model, to have children.

Nevertheless, when I think about my own social circle, in the broadest sense, I realise it encompasses blended families, single-parent families, families with same-sex parents, single mothers who have carried embryos other women froze earlier, single heterosexual women who have conceived children with their gay friends and raised them together, children raised in polyamorous households in which the parents have other partners, and more or less the full menu of options that are now available to us to form a family. But nowhere in this entire fertile, joyous cross section, evidence of the many ways we've found to come together, to love one another, am I able to find a single Anna, nor a single Nora.

I don't personally know a single mother who has voluntarily left her children to seek out her own identity, like Nora, or because she believes they don't fit into her life with a new partner, like Anna. And if I did, I imagine they would be surrounded by a scandal not so different from those Anna and Nora sparked in their literary universes.

No one would ostracise the abandoner, but at least a few would find the situation implausible, like the priest who rejected *A Doll's House*, and would assume something else was going on: a nervous breakdown, maybe, or a depressive episode; we would wish them good therapy, rest, medication. With the problem corrected or controlled, it would be natural, expected, for them to reunite. I suspect the opposite would strike us as a tragedy for the mother and the children. Of course, I'm talking about a circumstance that doesn't involve fleeing violence. I'm dismayed to find that within me, within my environment, the thinking would not be so different from that of Kitty or Dolly: conventional, resigned mothers from a novel like *Anna Karenina*, which Tolstoy conceived as a cautionary tale. I'm surprised that obtuse Torvald Helmer's arguments – 'motherless!' – haven't lost their validity, or at least not entirely.

Since I am also fond of reading 'in the dock with the criminal', as Virginia Woolf prefers, and as some students do on the

forums of websites selling essays about nineteenth-century literature, I like to imagine how Nora might have spent that first
night without her three children; if she smuggled one of their
shirts along so she could breathe in its scent, if she, too, felt a
brief flutter of excitement when she realised that she could eat
whatever she felt like for dinner and not what she had previously
assigned the cook, that she was free to do what she wanted for
the first time in her adult life. If she were afraid her children
would cry for her, or if what frightened her most that first night
was the opposite: the thought that her children might promptly
forget her instead.

What If?: The Braided Songs of Joni Mitchell and Vashti Bunyan

It's about one of the most painful experiences imaginable – giving a child up for adoption against your will – yet Joni Mitchell's devastating 'Little Green' also contains one of the most sarcastic verses in all of the seventies folk songbook. 'He's a nonconformer,' Mitchell tells the daughter she had to abandon, with more nonchalance than heartbreak. The nonconformer, who has left for California, 'hearing that everything's warmer there', was Brad MacMath, Mitchell's first boyfriend, a photographer she met at the Alberta College of Art and to whom she lost her virginity, almost immediately after which she became pregnant.

MacMath has gone down in history as the author of one of the most quoted and infamous break-up notes. The two young lovers had left school and moved to Toronto in the winter of 1964. They lived in a shared, dilapidated flat, one in which the previous tenants had used the banisters for firewood, to keep warm. When the couple found out Joni was pregnant, she decided not to have an abortion, and he disappeared for California, leaving behind a drawing of a pregnant woman gazing at the moon through a window, and the words: *The thief left it behind – the moon at the window.* Mitchell also made use of them a few years later, in her song 'Moon at the Window'.

Completely alone in a city that wasn't hers, and determined

not to tell her parents she was pregnant, the aspiring singer-songwriter found work in department stores. Since she couldn't afford the $170 fee to join the musicians' union, she could only play her repertoire at non-union clubs or the YMCA, where she made less money. She tried to find refuge in a home for single mothers, but they wouldn't accept her; there was no room. In 1965, the pill was not yet widely available, but the sexual revolution was, and Canadian social services weren't prepared to manage the flow of single mothers and children born out of wedlock.

Finally, in February 1965, alone in the Toronto hospital, Mitchell gave birth to a little blonde daughter she named Kelly Dale Anderson. Single mothers, like her, were treated like sinful criminals. They would bandage their breasts to decrease their milk supply and separate them from their babies, but Joni, whom almost everyone was still calling Joan, was permitted to spend ten days with her daughter at the hospital, due to medical complications.

Around the same time, in London, another young folk singer obsessed with Bob Dylan, a middle-class girl born in Ireland but raised in England, Jennifer Vashti Bunyan, met Andrew Loog Oldham, the manager of the Rolling Stones. Oldham was very pleased with the work he had done with Marianne Faithfull, whom he believed he had sold as the perfect pop doll, and wanted to repeat the trick with Jennifer, who was going by only Vashti. It would be several years before Faithfull fully freed herself as an artist. Oldham already had a blonde, now he also wanted a pretty brunette with a guitar. They released a single with a song by Mick Jagger and Keith Richards on side A and a song by Bunyan herself on side B, but neither this nor the next single had huge success.

In 1967, somewhat disillusioned with the music business and

seeing that no one was taking her seriously as a songwriter, Bunyan made a decision that seemed perfectly logical at the time: she set out on a trip through Britain in a cart pulled by horses, with her then-boyfriend, Robert Lewis. The couple had been sleeping under a rhododendron bush in a London park, and when the Bank of England, who owned the garden, evicted them from the area, they decided to buy the cart from a Roma family. The idea was to use the rickety vehicle to travel as far as the Hebrides, an archipelago off Scotland, where the singer-songwriter Donovan had established a commune. The musician had bought three remote islets on which he planned to organise a self-sufficient sanctuary, a place where his community of friends could practise free love and respect for the land.

Bunyan and Lewis's pilgrimage lasted a year and a half, and by the time they arrived at the archipelago, Donovan had gone, and the pastoral dream had ended, but Vashti had made good use of her time along the way. As they travelled the muddy highways of Great Britain in their horse-drawn cart, Bunyan composed the songs that would later comprise her album *Just Another Diamond Day*, a collection of unsettling ballads flecked with escapism, but also a kind of earthly lament, as if they had emerged from the tension between the dream of the commune and the reality of the highway.

Back in Canada, Joni Mitchell had already become a 'child with a child', as she sings in 'Little Green'. Social services pressured her to give the baby up for adoption, warning that the more time that passed, the more difficult it would be to find her a family. She resisted. During that time, she was staying with a friend in Calgary, Lorrie Wood, one of the few people who knew her secret. Wood was able to understand her situation perfectly, because she herself had become pregnant as a single woman and had given her child up for adoption. 'It was the best thing I ever did,' her friend insisted. 'You can't put yourself in it. It's selfish. You have to be beyond it.' Joni looked at her daughter, who resembled her so much, and thought: a little longer. Eventually, she did put her in foster care.

The singer believed she had found the solution to her problems in Chuck Mitchell, another singer-songwriter, slightly older (he was twenty-nine at the time), whom she met at the club The Penny Farthing when he critiqued her cover of Bob Dylan's 'Mr. Tambourine Man'. Chuck Mitchell had a union card, which meant they could sing as a duo, and a US passport. He seemed to offer the perfect way out. Thirty-six hours after they met, they decided to get married. The plan was to go to Detroit, enter the music scene there, And, once they had enough money, 'get the baby out of the hock', as the singer told her biographer David Yaffe.

None of that happened. Chuck Mitchell, who came from an upper-middle-class family and had attended an elite college, saw his new wife as an exotic and somewhat untamed creature. It wasn't long before he made clear he had no intention of raising another man's child. On one of their trips from Detroit to Toronto, they went to the home where the girl was staying, took turns holding her, first Chuck, then Joni, and said goodbye. Joni signed the papers renouncing her custody. They chose what is known as a 'closed adoption', which means she didn't leave her name, only some facts. That the father had been tall, and the mother, too. That the mother was from Saskatchewan and was leaving the baby to go to the United States and 'pursue career as folk singer'.

In England, Vashti Bunyan also found herself pregnant, with no home and a promising but erratic music career. The producer Joe Boyd, one of the best-connected men in the business, had invited her to record the songs she had been composing over the course of her hippie pilgrimage. The team that was to play on the album was stellar, which explains, in part, why these recordings have not been lost to history. Performing Vashti's songs were members of the Incredible String Band, and producing and playing the violin, banjo, and mandolin was Robert Kirby, who had just worked with another British folk prodigy, Nick Drake. At the start, the young songwriter was unimpressed with the names. 'I was so far removed from anything to do with music in 1968 and '69 – going from having been almost obsessively interested in it before, to being cut off without radio or TV or music papers (no electricity – little money) – that I didn't even know who they were!' she said later in an interview. Still, they recorded that singular album, and shortly after, Vashti learned she was pregnant. She had to decide what to do with her life. She could stay in London to promote her music, or she could go back to the Hebrides, where the dream of a communal life seemed to have died already. Eventually, she and Robert decided they would take the child, Leif, to another commune, which the members of the Incredible String Band had formed on the border between England and Scotland.

The album was released in 1970, but to little fanfare. It was lost in the profusion of excellent music produced in those years, maybe too strange, too confessional, too feminine. Someone said the songs sounded like children's lullabies. After that point, Vashti considered her musical story over. She went from the commune to a farm in Ireland. After Leif, she had another son, and later on, a third. She also raised three stepchildren. She didn't touch a guitar for thirty years, not even incidentally, and she never listened to her own recordings. In fact, she didn't own even one copy of *Just Another Diamond Day*. She had given them all away.

Joni Mitchell, on the other hand, no longer had the burden of a baby as her career began to take off. It's funny, and a little bleak, to read how Chuck and Joni Mitchell described those years to Yaffe, author of the book *Reckless Daughter: A Portrait of Joni Mitchell.*

He says:

We were both talented, remember that, if in quite different ways. It was fun, and a lot of things were happening at once; songs getting written, tunings found, clothes sewn, curtains fashioned and hung, estate sales and auctions and roast beef and Yorkshire pudding and green beans and all-night card games and soirees with troubadours (a.k.a. hustling songs at the local clubs). It was. a. great. scene.

She says: 'Chuck Mitchell was my first major exploiter, a complete asshole.'

It seems clear enough who was sewing the curtains and making the Yorkshire pudding – and finding the best melodies, for that matter.

The marriage dissolved after two years. Oddly, Joni, on the verge of leaving her husband, took his last name to perform under, to construct a new identity for herself as a singer-songwriter with her own repertoire, no longer dependent on endless covers of Joan Baez and Pete Seeger. Three years after giving up her child, Mitchell had a record deal, a car and a house, a permanent place in the group of musicians that made their homes in Laurel Canyon. In the considerable record of writings on that milieu, anecdotes abound about how Joni Mitchell's enormous talent confused the male musicians and songwriters. Like the time when Eric Clapton stopped over in Laurel Canyon and Neil Young told him: you have to hear the girl who lives in the flat upstairs. Joni played for them, and even a guy with the diamantine self-esteem of Eric Clapton had to admit that this woman was able to do things no one else could.

At almost all her concerts, she sang 'Little Green', which had become an essential part of her songbook. She played it when she made her debut on Bleecker Street, the mythical land of the New York folkies; she played it on Canadian TV. It was all there. The lyrics were transparent: they discuss signing papers in the family name; how the person was sad and sorry but not ashamed. They entreat Little Green to have a happy ending.

But no one knew or wanted to figure out what Joni Mitchell was singing about in that song. When, finally, in 1971, she released the song on the album *Blue*, which would catapult and cement her reputation as one of the great composers of her generation, a large portion of the public still didn't understand. A *Rolling Stone* critic lamented that the lyric is 'pretty' and 'poetic' but 'dressed up in such cryptic references that it passeth all understanding'. Mitchell later explained that this song and others were her way of sending messages to her lost daughter.

After almost thirty years, in a novel-like twist, mother and daughter reunited. Each had been looking for the other for some time. Kelly Dale was now Kilauren Gibb, a name given to her by her parents, two teachers in a comfortable suburb of Toronto, when they adopted her at six months, the same day Joni Mitchell signed the papers she refers to in 'Little Green'. Kilauren had worked as a model and was, at that point, in graduate school. Although her friends had told her when she was a teenager that she was adopted, Gibb didn't have confirmation from her parents until she turned twenty-seven and she herself was pregnant. Then she looked for information about her biological parents and found the famous note that said her mother was born in Saskatchewan and had gone to the US to try her luck as a folk singer. Any half-fan of Joni Mitchell could have connected the dots, but it was another four years before Gibb put together the puzzle, with the unwitting help of one of the singer's art-school roommates, who sold the story of Joni Mitchell's 'illegitimate child' to a tabloid.

The singer hesitantly admitted that the story was true in some interviews, and she began to receive letters from blonde Canadian girls claiming to be her daughter. None of them fit, until, in 1997, a note arrived from Kilauren, along with some documentation. It was clear that Kilauren was Kelly Dale.

Mitchell sent plane tickets for her and her son, Marlin. After more than thirty years, she would reunite with her daughter and meet her first grandchild while she was at it. The reconciliation was probably much more public than she had imagined. The story, so scandalous, was all over the news. Oprah Winfrey, Barbara Walters, and Larry King requested interviews. Kilauren had her boyfriend act as her publicist, requesting ten thousand dollars for every meeting with journalists. People who saw Joni Mitchell during that time recall that she was radiant, that nothing mattered to her but the daughter she had recovered. In photos taken for the interviews they gave together, they hold their faces close, as if to confirm their resemblance. The same impossibly high cheekbones, the same straight hair, each looking sidelong at the other, incredulous.

The romance of the reunion was short-lived. Soon, tensions surged, in part due to media pressure and Kilauren's interest in making money off their story. By 2001, their relationship had become so fraught, with so many harsh words exchanged, that they mutually decided to break it off, and didn't pick it back up again until 2013. According to Joni, the abandonment had traumatised Kilauren, and she used the grandchildren to carry out emotional blackmail, an accusation that Kilauren has always denied.

Those years of reconnection with her daughter also brought a certain disconnection from music. During that time, Mitchell was focused on painting. In a piece Zadie Smith wrote about her for *The New Yorker*, the novelist ponders why Joni Mitchell would rather be 'a perfectly nice painter than a singer touched by the sublime'. Smith speculates that in rejecting what she did best, perhaps Mitchell sought to protect herself from the expectations of her audience. It's always easier, of course, to move through the world with a fair dose of talent. When one surpasses a certain quantity, that's when things get complicated.

If Joni Mitchell spent thirty years with music, without her daughter, Vashti Bunyan experienced just the opposite: she devoted thirty years to her children, and then music came out to meet her again. Around the start of this century, Bunyan, almost sixty years old, started to google herself. That's how she learned her name was an especially precious commodity among those in search of musical rarities. For some time, Vashti had been getting emails from bearded strangers – like Devendra Banhart – declaring their love for her, saying her songs clawed at their souls. In 2000, a small but influential label, Spinney, had reissued *Just Another Diamond Day*, and the album had finally found its natural audience. Soon, Piano Magic, Cocteau Twins, and Animal Collective threw themselves at her feet. Vashti Bunyan's second musical life arose in part because of the snobbishness of those who said they adored her – oh, you haven't listened to Vashti Bunyan? – but even so, it was a clear case of reparation, a timely rescue for a woman who'd squandered her gift and, for once, wouldn't have to wait until death to be recognised.

Her songs, especially the ones on *Just Another Diamond Day*, written while she travelled through the British Isles in a horse-drawn cart, no longer seemed insignificant. They could be appreciated for what they were: delicate, uncommon mechanisms. Urged on by her sudden popularity in the indie sphere, Bunyan picked up her guitar and began to compose again, signed a contract with a record label, re-entered the recording studio, and started producing from home.

In 2005, Bunyan said in the magazine *Perfect Sound Forever*:

Recording is different [now]. I'm not stuck in a glass box, unable to make any contribution to the way things sound, for a start. Recording was the thing I always loved best, and so to be back in a studio again is so very good. Better though is my computer, and music programs, which mean I can lock myself away and play with all the technology that fascinated me but was denied me back then – because I was a shy girl or because singers had no say in production or whatever.

They also asked about her children, who knew very little about their mother's musical history, and she responded with this: 'I'd like to have something to leave for my children, even if it is just songs. Sounds a bit daft, I guess, but I hid my musical story from them for so long, and now I'd like them to know it.'

In that 'daft', and that 'I guess', you can make out: forgive me if I sound like a mother. It's a standard register, an apologetic tone that's less frequent, even rare, in new fathers, who launch into emotional talk of their children without going into raptures. It's still difficult for women to practise that very specific poetry. At any moment they might be accused of sentimentality, or worse.

When Joni Mitchell talks about the sixties in interviews, there's something she always wants to point out: she did not leave her daughter for music. 'But let's clear up something that people assume erroneously, and I see it written again and again and again,' she said firmly to a Canadian TV reporter:

That I gave up my daughter to further my career. This is so wrong. There was no career. My music at that point – first of all, I was just a folksinger. It was just – it was just – there was no ambition, there was no – you know, I had a nice voice, I guess, I played OK, you know, but there was no real gift that – it was just something that was happening, that was going to die out soon, you know? It was a way to get money to smoke, you know, and have a pizza and go to a movie. And to bowl. Because that's what I did at art school too. I came in there with no frills. I had to earn half my fare to art school because my parents disapproved, and there was nothing left over. So singing in the clubs was fun, and it afforded me a little bit of income that I wouldn't have had.

In the same interview, she repeats that she was living in poverty in 1965 and would have had no way to care for the baby. She also recalls her first husband, the 'complete asshole'. And she thanks him for that awful marriage, which at least provided material she could use for her first good songs.

While Vashti Bunyan, Joni Mitchell, and other women musicians stumbled in different but almost always painful ways against the reality that it wouldn't be so easy for them to have children, raise them, and also devote themselves to music, their male counterparts continued to accumulate children, albums, and marriages at an easy but steady rhythm.

Bob Dylan, whom both women had idolised in their youth, had six children, five biological and one he adopted, from the marriage of his first wife, Sara Lownds. David Crosby adds six more. Graham Nash, to continue the list of Joni Mitchell's ex-lovers, stopped at three, the same number as Neil Young, one from an extramarital relationship. His ex-wife, the singer-songwriter Pegi Young, who left music to raise their eldest son, Ben, born with cerebral palsy, recorded an album when Neil Young left her for the actress Daryl Hannah. The track list reads like a manual about how to rebound from a painful break-up: 'Gave My Best to You', 'Too Little, Too Late', 'You Won't Take My Laugh Away from Me', 'Up to Here', and 'Trying to Live My Life Without You'.

Reading the stories of Joni Mitchell and Vashti Bunyan in parallel invites us back to the ever-tempting childhood game of 'What if?' What if Mitchell had kept her baby, maybe telling her parents the truth, as she would many years later? Here, we can surrender to speculative fiction and imagine Joni Mitchell as a housewife, or a drawing instructor in Saskatchewan. Playing her guitar at parties, her old repertoire, copied from Joan Baez. That would be a world without 'Little Green', which wouldn't have cause to exist anymore, without 'Blue' and without 'Ladies of the Canyon'.

'What if Vashti Bunyan had been determined to keep writing and performing?' we might also ask ourselves. Well, there's Carole King, the Meryl Streep of music, who had four children from two marriages and a fabulous career. But there aren't many other examples. As a general rule, you couldn't raise children and also sing.

You don't have to be a singer-songwriter or be touched by the sublime, in the words of Zadie Smith, to play 'What if?' Anyone can do that from the comfort of her home and in the perfect mediocrity of her existence. If you want to apply a bit of scientific method to the matter, have data on hand. A woman with children who wants to imagine how her life might be without them knows, for example, that in that parallel reality, she would be making on average 30 per cent more. The Bank of Spain says so. She would also be spending 100 per cent less on things as expensive as school lunches and paediatric dentistry, so right from the start, her disposable income would be much higher, whatever her salary range.

Despite this, 'What if I hadn't had children?' is a form of 'What if?' frequently practised in private and silence, on nights of fitful sleep, when the woman who is a mother compares herself with her non-mother friends. Those friends, with their lives and their hips intact, with their constant flow of new places, new lovers, with their universe still in expansion. In the eyes of the woman who is a mother, whose life has become so narrow, the days lived by her friends without children seem impossibly versatile; their skin seems tauter, their hair shinier. The friends without children, when they want to go to the cinema, just get up, buy tickets, and go to the cinema. Their pelvic floors are still pristine. They haven't had to go to post-partum classes at a public health centre, with twenty other women in leggings suffering various grades of incontinence. That kind of defeat is foreign to them.

Life with children provides other kinds of stimulation. Creatures who clamber into bed with you in the morning, their bodies still warm from sleep, and tell you, as if it were any old thing, that they 'love you to infinity'. But it's also a life that almost always moves within a limited geography. When you have children, the number of streets in which your new life exists shrinks, surely by even more than that 30 per cent decrease in your salary. There always comes a day when the woman who is a mother finds herself in an area of her city she used to frequent, in her old life, and she's overwhelmed with bewilderment. So these streets are still here, and all these people walk them daily. How strange.

I don't often go far with 'What if?' Because immediately I come up against the reality of two children who already exist, who have induced in me a superhuman love. I understand that this can also go the opposite way, with even the people who are the most confident in their decision not to have children occasionally giving in to that 'What if?', so prickly and so definitive, the biggest 'What if?' of all, higher up on the ladder of 'What if?'s than partners we discarded, cities we didn't move to, and jobs we didn't accept.

'Little Green', of course, is also, in part, a sad form of 'What if?'

In those years when Joni Mitchell was often imagining what her lost daughter might be like – she never stopped – she wrote a melancholy song that also allowed her to envision the life the daughter might be living, where she pictured northern lights, icicles, birthday clothes – but also, sometimes, sorrow.

It's the Mother's Fault

'It's the mother's fault' is an idea that travels well. It could have been uttered at any moment in history, applied either to one specific mother, or to mothers as a social construct. 'It's the mother's fault,' we think almost unconsciously, streaming a documentary one Saturday night, one of those perfectly calibrated audio-visual products that guides viewers so we know when to flinch, when to be surprised, when to be indignant. After watching something like that, we go to sleep knowing we've just passed through a full range of prescribed emotions, ending with a moral certitude as comforting as the blanket on the sofa. In the Michael Jackson documentary *Leaving Neverland*, for example, everything is set up so the viewer will loathe the mothers of the two children he abused, groupies dazzled by money and fame who practically handed their sons over in exchange for access to their idol. Maybe that's not what they were, but it is how they're portrayed.

It's the mother's fault for not being vigilant enough, we still think every time there's another harrowing case of child disappearance, a child who falls into a well, for example, or a child who disappears one afternoon with a stranger, like in the stories. It's the mother's fault – she wanted her son to be famous, and look how that turned out, we might think witnessing the spectacle of any child prodigy gone bad, although in that area, tyrannical and exploitative fathers – of Tiger Woods, for example, or the Williams sisters, the Jacksons themselves, Britney Spears – tend to monopolise public punishment. In those cases, the mothers are charged as accomplices, for not having known to protect their offspring from exploitation.

This sinister thread can also be traced through medical and sociological history: the many ways they've found to offload almost anything onto mothers. In social science, it's quite common to mock today what everyone believed yesterday. How could we have fallen for that? we think, not suspecting that in fifty years' time, the same judgement will come of some theories that are right now perfectly embedded in the ideological hardware of our era. The truth is, every historical period finds its way of sentencing mothers, and if one thing remains unchanged through all of history, it's the profound belief that guilt almost always lies with her.

During the first half of the twentieth century, for example, there was a general belief that mothers with psychological problems would give birth to healthy children only to literally drive them mad. Freudian theory had spread the hypothesis that schizophrenia was caused either by mothers who were too cold, or by mothers who were too protective. A study published in 1934 analysed the environments of forty-five children who had been diagnosed with schizophrenia, though today it's likely they would have received a wide range of diagnoses. Among those forty-five children, the doctors leading the study found two cases of what they called 'maternal rejection' and thirty-three cases of 'maternal overprotection', and with that, the idea that both rejection and excessive attachment could give rise to mental illness in children was solidified.

In 1948, a psychiatrist named Frieda Fromm-Reichmann

christened these mothers 'schizophrenogenic', agents of illness, and wrote in one of her papers, 'the schizophrenic is painfully distrustful and resentful of other people, due to the severe early warp and rejection he encountered in important people of his infancy and childhood, as a rule, mainly in a schizophrenogenic mother.' This philosophy remained prevalent for decades. At the end of the sixties, a grandchild of Sigmund Freud, Sophie Freud, trained as a psychiatric social worker in Boston and was surprised by the profession's hostility towards the parents of children on the autism spectrum. Decades later, she wrote that the staff were well-intentioned and wanted to help, but their theoretical framework led them to draw absurd and vicious conclusions. Conclusions whose origins could be traced right through her own family tree. The psychoanalytic miscellany, that compendium of offshoots that at times seem to veer almost completely from Freud's original theories, ended up crystallising into a special dislike of and cruelty towards The Mother all throughout the twentieth century.

For a time, there was no limit to what an imaginative mind could do armed with the theories of Freud and Jung. Take Philip Wylie, for example, a classic product of the schools where the East Coast elite sent their children in the twenties and thirties. The schools Richard Yates describes in his novels, where upper-class children are taught leadership, stoicism, and social impairment. Wylie went to Exeter, the same school as famous alumni Mark Zuckerberg, John Irving, Gore Vidal, and various Rockefellers.

Wylie had vague literary ambitions and wrote several science fiction novels after graduating from college. But he did not find success until 1942, when he devised one of the most ridiculous, fascinating, and destructive pop-psychology phenomena of the period, which he called 'momism'. Armed with the spirited and sabre-rattling language of the time, he expounded on the term in a book called *Generation of Vipers*. In it, he singled out a group responsible for the ruin of US soldiers, as powerful as the Luftwaffe, with the precision of all the Axis powers combined. These were American mothers, women who were 'ridiculous, vain, vicious, a little mad', 'reckless and unreasoning', who had converted an entire crop of young men into a band of cowards, if not homosexuals, men who were dying like moths on the front because they hadn't been raised under the right conditions.

Commercial rationale might lead us to believe that his pamphlet, which attacks the military establishment by laying into the mother, should have failed amid the patriotic fervour that was, at the time, flourishing in the US. But both the publishing market and the collective psyche can be unpredictable, and the book became an influential bestseller that shipped fifty thousand copies between 1943 and 1955 and had a much more enduring long-tail.

Wylie invented an acronym that stood for everything he hated: LIE, 'Liberal Intellectual Establishment'. Emboldened by this theoretical framework of his own creation, he sat the entire country down on the sofa and diagnosed a clear case of the Oedipus complex that could only be treated with pseudo-Jungian ideas. With its references to the 'enwhorement of American womanhood', its cheap tabloid alliteration, and its feverish syntagms ('megaloid momworship', 'spiritual saboteurs'), *Generation of Vipers* is hard to read today. 'Thus the women of America raped the men, not sexually, unfortunately, but morally, since neuters come hard by morals,' Wylie writes.

In time, the book was not only commercially successful, but also well reviewed by critics as influential as the writer Malcolm Cowley. Simone de Beauvoir, who had her own issues with the subject of motherhood, said Wylie had done a brilliant analysis of the reign of the matriarch in American society. The idea of momism quickly filtered into popular culture and left seeds that germinated over the course of decades. We see it in movies like *Psycho*: Norman Bates is the definitive victim of momism.

In the years after Wylie's book was published, several like it appeared, bolstering his theory on the noxious effects of a hyper-present, paralysing mother. His philosophy seeped through the cracks into dominant discourse, as feminist professor Stephanie Coontz has shown in her scholarship. When the military psychiatrist Edward A. Strecker went back to the front, where he was met with too many emotionally unstable soldiers, he wrote *Their Mother's Sons*, another pamphlet targeting 'moms' – Strecker draws a distinction between young men who still call their mothers 'mom' and those who have graduated to the more adult and sombre 'mother' – and the culture that had allowed a bunch of cry-babies to go off and fight in Europe. Strecker, of course, also blamed the mothers for their sons' homosexuality, an idea that has managed to find its subscribers throughout history. Even Betty Friedan endorses it in *The Feminine Mystique*, the foundational text for second-wave feminism that hasn't exactly aged well.

These pathological mothers have convinced their male sons that they will never find a woman as good as they themselves are and, in parallel, have instructed them that heterosexual coitus is an inherently violent act in which the man is the beast and the woman the victim. 'By her actions and what she has said and implied, [she] has poisoned the boy's mind against normal, mature heterosexual living,' concludes Strecker, whose book was not as successful as Wylie's, though it did influence military psychiatry and civilian clinical practices.

Four years after *Generation of Vipers*, another pop-psychology bestseller, *Modern Woman: The Lost Sex*, flung out a figure pulled from who knows what study: that two thirds of Americans were neurotic, and the cause was right at home, in the kitchen, to be exact, and responded to the name 'mom'. The stereotype crossed into the fifties, fertilised and healthy, and carried on long after, with hundreds of literary and filmic representations of shrill matriarchs and castrated husbands, which have also allowed for various cultural specificities, like the Italian *mamma*, and the hyper-protective Yiddish *mama* we know from Philip Roth novels and Woody Allen movies, who reminds us so much of the Almodóvarian *mamá*.

Around the same time Philip Wylie constructed his 'momist' theory, the Austrian psychiatrist Leo Kanner developed a different but complementary idea, which would not be refuted for years. Kanner coined the concept of the 'refrigerator mother', so cold and aseptic as to have caused her child's autism. Oppressive mothers made their male children unwell or gay, but absent mothers made them autistic. Again, the idea has its roots in interpretations of Freudian theories. Kanner and Hans Asperger, the doctor who gave his name to the syndrome that is a form of autism, mostly studied cases occurring in upper-class families, many of them in the academic sphere, and concluded that even if the causes of these conditions were known to be mostly genetic, an uncaring mother could contribute to their development in her children. The narrowness of their study also led them to a fallacy, since they deduced that cases of autism were more common in highly intelligent families.

Later, another child development researcher, Bruno Bettelheim, expounded on the term with an analogy that, at that time, set off every kind of alarm, but also ensured the whole world would pay attention. He said 'refrigerator mothers' were like the guards at Nazi concentration camps. He himself was Jewish and a victim of the Holocaust, imprisoned in Dachau for ten months, so he believed he had the ethical privilege to make such a claim. 'The difference between the plight of prisoners in a concentration camp and the conditions which lead to autism and schizophrenia in children is, of course, that the child has never had a previous chance to develop much of a personality,' he wrote in his book *The Empty Fortress: Infantile Autism and the Birth of the Self*, which, while academic, had a smooth and accessible style that earned it some popularity.

In fact, that was what made Bettelheim's theory, and Bettelheim himself, so dangerous. Charismatic and extremely media friendly, the psychiatrist, who after the war settled into a professorship at the University of Chicago, appeared frequently in the press and had a natural gift for self-promotion, so his theories circulated rapidly and dominated the study of autism until far into the sixties. When he was interviewed by *Time* in 1969, he said that 'refrigerator mothers' had managed to 'defrost just enough to produce a son'. A claim like that was well received in those years, when the word 'frigid' was in the air. There was one thing the Eisenhower suburbanites – the famous men in grey suits who took the car to work every day – and those who first embraced the counterculture could fully agree on: nobody wanted an icy wife. There was nothing worse than a frigid woman.

Bettelheim may have caused long-range damage to women and mothers with his influence, but the harm he inflicted on patients at the Orthogenic School was much more bodily and concrete. He directed the school from 1944 until the early seventies, deploying a racist, almost eugenic policy (he didn't accept non-white children until he was forced to). Right at the start of his tenure, he stopped accepting children with epilepsy and cerebral palsy, who had previously made up the bulk of the patient population, arguing that those conditions could already be treated at home. He focused instead on minors diagnosed as autistic, who would be likely to receive a wide range of diagnoses today, and who were brilliant on the academic side but faced emotional difficulties. He theorised that the children with autism actually had no pathology; they'd simply developed their behaviour in reaction to being brought up in miniature versions of concentration camps, almost always with a passive father and a refrigerator mother whose resentment of her femininity led her to desire her own child's death. As bizarre as it sounds, this account was fully accepted in mainstream psychiatry in the United States and Europe and had an even greater impact in South Korea.

The coldness of those mothers showed itself in repressed desires and an excessively modest behaviour in the home. A mother who locks the door when she goes to the bathroom, for example, is a potential 'refrigerator mother'. At the school, Bettelheim advocated for almost complete family separation, with the children who were admitted barely seeing their parents and remaining at the centre in the care of young women called 'instant mothers', who had to be accommodating, agreeable, and expressive.

In 1990, after being partially paralysed by a stroke, Bettelheim took his life by suffocating himself with a plastic bag. He was eighty-six years old. After his death, stories came to light of his abuses at the Orthogenic School, where an atmosphere of terror and oppression reigned. Several residents have published heartbreaking memoirs of their experiences, describing a looming, mercurial Bettelheim who dressed as Santa Claus for Christmas – he was a secular Jew so drawn to hyper-assimilation that he fell into self-loathing, and Christmas was the only holiday celebrated extravagantly at the centre – and who pulled boys from the showers by the hair to beat them in front of all their friends.

In 1997, Richard Pollak, an author whose brother had died as a child at the Orthogenic School, wrote a biography, *The Creation of Doctor B*, intending to discredit him forever, and to a certain extent, he succeeded. Today, no one defends his methods or his research, which has also been tarnished due to evidence of plagiarism found in some of his studies. But dismantling an idea is much harder than cancelling a person. And the possibility that a refrigerator mother, or even a microwave mother, who only warms superficially, without reaching the centre, could be the principal cause of a child's disorders would continue to find a place in popular culture for many years. Even now, it retains some validity, coupled as it is with the popular collective belief that it's always the mother's fault.

At the end of the eighties, two Canadian psychologists studied one hundred and twenty-five articles about children's mental health published in scientific magazines and found that seventy-two of them held mothers responsible for all kinds of psychological disorders: agoraphobia, hyperactivity, schizophrenia, and something called, criminally, 'homicidal transsexualism'. There was even a 1987 study that tied young girls' poor grades in mathematics to their mothers. A mother's guilt, like energy, cannot be created or destroyed, it can only be transformed.

Now, we read new epigenetic studies every week, linking a mother's obesity during pregnancy with the future obesity of her child, a mother's stress with her child's probable anxiety. Even levels of environmental pollution, they tell us, affect the foetus. So it's possible, even reasonable, to feel guilty for crossing streets in heavy traffic while pregnant, because the child's lungs may be compromised as you're simply strolling along the pavement. From the outset, all these studies are presented and accepted as sterile pieces of information, derived by the evolution of science to better the health of the unborn. What could prenatal medicine have to do with maternal guilt? No one is suspicious. It's just science, after all.

Sarah Richardson, a professor of science and gender studies at Harvard, has made this topic her speciality. In various academic papers and her book, *The Maternal Imprint*, she argues that many studies of 'the foetal programming hypothesis' are cryptic, and that the scientific community is often too quick to draw conclusions. Richardson has spent years denouncing the headlines taken from many medical studies, lines like 'maternal diet during pregnancy induces gene expression', 'grandma's experiences leave a mark on your genes', 'pregnant 9/11 survivors transmitted trauma to their children'. She and other researchers like her suggest someone should remember the fathers from time to time, since they also contribute to the foetuses, and these findings shouldn't only be used to single out mothers. A working-class mother doing twelve-hour shifts during her pregnancy and grabbing something from McDonald's on her way home has little use for a lecture regarding her diet and lack of rest.

The idea that what women do may leave a biological trace on their offspring before they're born went from being considered unscientific – except in the case of a serious accident or extreme conditions – to being fully accepted in a very short period, scientifically speaking, Richardson also explains. Before, a child's future was thought to be determined by a combination of genes and upbringing. That consensus was dismantled, and now, the field of intrauterine research has implications, most of them beneficial, for medicine, public health, psychology, biology, and genomics. In just thirty years, we have come to accept that everything a woman does, smokes, eats, breathes, touches, or experiences during her pregnancy can have consequences for her offspring, but we've barely paused to reflect on the socio-psychological effects of all these discoveries, which return the pregnant mother to a position of sole responsibility.

The guilt lies with the mother even before she is one. All women find that instinctively when they take a pregnancy test and think immediately of the three glasses of wine they had the night before, suspecting that in doing so, they've already damaged the foetus's brain. They are not even mothers yet, not even close, but they're already familiar with that special flavour of maternal remorse.

The very low birth rates in almost all developed countries is always – correctly – attributed to agreed-upon tangible factors. How much it costs to have children. The absence of a social fabric within which it is possible to raise them in a slightly less individualistic way, not the way we do now, as if each family were privately investing in their human assets with the hope of maximising yield in the form of healthy, happy, and successful children.

The effects of romantic capitalism also contribute to the fact that fewer children are being born. It's difficult for women to decide whom to reproduce with – there are so many options out there – and even more difficult for them to decide whether to do so alone, a choice that requires multiplying all the existing negative variables (greater expenses, more aloneness, more anxiety). But there's something else to take into account when considering the growing ambivalence among women, the fact that more and more of them are spending their last fertile years consumed by the anguish of doubt – to have children or not to have children. Their intimate understanding, their awareness that, if the step is taken, if the woman becomes a mother, someone will be prepared to hurl all manner of epithets her way in the name of science. Obese mother; refrigerator mother; behaviourist mother, counting hours between feedings and planning toilet training with the help of an Excel spreadsheet; a mother who's too attached, who takes her baby everywhere and breastfeeds until he's five; a helicopter mother, who hovers around her little one day and night and deafens her with the noise of her rotating blades. Each one will carry her own specific ration of guilt for whatever harm might befall her children.

I've never had a clear idea of what category I belong to. Too absent-minded to helicopter, not momist enough to be a marsupial mum.

'You cried, right?' many people asked me when I took my older son to day nursery for the first time. They asked me again four years later, when it was the younger one's turn. 'A little bit,' I lied.

The truth is, I didn't cry. I felt too grateful and relieved. Each kid was about seven months old when it happened, and I'd been back at work for at least four or five, trying to write and do interviews and send invoices with a baby on top of me, a baby who always, invariably, awoke from his nap and started crying when I was in the middle of a call with someone in Los Angeles, the organisation of which had required ten emails with fifteen people copied in on each one. During those post-partum months when I had no choice but to work, I was overwhelmed with distraction, exhaustion, anxiety. And, if I stopped for a second, I noticed the holes in my brain were enlarging, that it had turned into a kind of slotted spoon through which slipped all the good ideas I should have been having. Was it just me, or was I incapable of coming up with verbs? I was convinced I had used adverbs with greater finesse before. Maybe with my placenta I had also lost my grasp of language.

So no, I didn't cry on the first day of nursery for either son, turning them over to people perfectly capable of caring for them, with more time, resources, and patience, who would return them to me a few hours later, clean, happy, and fed.

I fear I'm not a crocodile mum, either – the kind who transports her children in her mouth, warming them with her breath. How could I share breath when sometimes I don't have enough for myself? A tow-truck mother? I think that sometimes, when I'm pushing a buggy uphill with one hand, reaching out with the other to guide a scooter. Each machine, as my elder son used to call them, carrying a temporary resident. I stretch my arms into a T, bow down in an ancestral gesture, and self-dramatise a little. Look at you, turned into a minivan, I think, as if I'm watching from outside myself, from the future, or someone is taking a video.

Here we come, the poor leopard mothers, I thought for a while, walking up to the nursery – the neighbourhood where I live always seemed flat until I had children and started pushing along an old pram, but there's nothing flat about it, it's all uphill. I had, and have, a skirt that falls a hand's length below my knees. It closes with a tie, like a sarong, and it's printed with little leopard spots. It's quite forgiving, an expression that always strikes me as funny when used in reference to clothing. In the seventeen minutes it took to make that trip (twenty-one if I had bad luck with pedestrian crossings or had to pause to pick up toys that fell from the buggy), I used to see three or four women wearing exactly the same skirt, which cost me twenty-five euros at the chain Oysho. I also crossed paths, each morning and each afternoon, with leopard mothers in very similar models, from Zara or H&M. It was a skirt that, worn at that moment, said: 'I haven't entirely abandoned who I was, I'm making an effort to look like my old self.' And at the same time: 'I only have twenty-five euros for nonessentials, you better not look at my eyebrows, my new hips and I are still getting to know each other, don't ask too much, pass me over, be forgiving.'

In short, it was – is – a skirt that can compromise, shape-giving but not too tight, offering the spirit of consensus in the battle raging between who you used to be and who you are. 'Now that we were mothers we were all shadows of our former selves, chased by the women we used to be before we had children. We didn't really know what to do with her, this fierce, independent young woman who followed us about, shouting and pointing the finger while we wheeled our buggies in the English rain,' Deborah Levy writes in *Things I Don't Want to Know: On Writing*. When I read it, I felt it had been written for me, and proceeded to swap in 'Barcelona's smothering July sun' for 'the English rain'.

Leopards without claws, I thought as I walked uphill. Often, pushing along the buggy, I nodded at another feline out of inertia, a stranger. Shouldn't members of the same group support one another this way?

The peculiar decision is not *not* having children in these conditions, nor finding it so hard to decide to do so; the peculiar thing is that so many people continue, we continue, signing the Faustian bargain. Do you want children? Well, good choice. They're soft, they smell good until they smell bad, they'll squeeze your hand when they hear a motorcycle or step into the ocean (I'm here, protect me), and in just three years, they'll have the ability to utter brilliant and absurd aphorisms, like miniature Lewis Carrolls, fabulous nonsense you'll need to write down because you don't ever want to forget it.

If you want all that (and how could you not, it's the best thing in the world), you should know each baby arrives with its portion of guilt, a significant one, and you can't have one thing without the other. You'll see. You can also leave, but almost no one does.

Maria Montessori:
The Child and the Method

These people pay a lot for mud, I think to myself every week while I wait for my elder son to come out of his after-school club, in a neighbourhood that's already on its third or fourth round of gentrification. One of the other kids usually looks especially dirty, covered in earth. Since the child is wearing a tracksuit from a Montessori school that costs some twelve hundred euros per month, food and transportation included, plus two thousand for matriculation and a security deposit of six hundred – I googled it, I'm that kind of person – I calculate that each streak of dirt petrified on his trouser legs costs this family a small fortune. But, I think, killing time near the door where my own son will soon appear, reasonably clean, they must have expected that. Those serious stains are also proof that their kid has spent the day rolling around outside, not sitting in a classroom like the children of the poor.

There are Montessori schools all over the world, almost all private and most very expensive, as well as a parallel multimillion-dollar business built on Montessori products and comprising multiple items, from blocks that light up, to sandboxes and puzzles, to knives designed so the children can use them un-supervised. In general, any object with the Montessori tag is automatically 40 per cent more expensive than its non-Montessori equivalent.

Some who study the method have pointed out the paradox that a revolutionary pedagogue, who first tested out her approach on the children of the working class in the San Lorenzo neighbourhood in Rome, ended up giving her name to what is now, in practice, essentially for the elite. One of richest men in the world, Jeff Bezos, studied at a Montessori school and often says that without that education, he never would have founded Amazon. Now, he himself is opening Montessori academies in the United States. Larry Page and Sergey Brin, of Google, were also Montessori kids. These facts are available in some two hundred articles on the internet, with titles like 'What do all these multimillionaires have in common?'

Many Montessori-trained teachers lament the bastardisation of the brand. That's not what Montessori is, they insist. The same educators would be shocked if they joined a text chain of middle-class mums and saw how casually the word 'Montessori' is thrown around, now that it has been absorbed by the somewhat appalling force that is parenting humour. 'I'm total Montessori,' we say when we've just committed an old-fashioned, counterproductive disciplinary act, like telling the child he'll have to repeat fifth grade if he doesn't stop writing letters backwards. Or, 'Well look on the bright side, at least he's Montessori,' we say when the child breaks a toy he has just been given. The Italian educator said the most natural thing a child can do with a toy is try and destroy it to see what's inside.

Before she became a bad joke, an educational approach, and a very lucrative brand, Maria Montessori was a woman, a woman who was complex, erudite, and far ahead of her time, and a mother who couldn't try out her method on her own son, since she wasn't present for his childhood.

The future pedagogue gave birth to her only child, Mario, when she was still working in medicine. In 1898, Maria was twenty-eight years old and had achieved what very few women in Italy had up to that point: she had become a doctor and was specialising in paediatrics. She had just defended her thesis and was already codirecting a hospital for children who at that time were called 'mentally handicapped', a tag that bunched together all special educational needs. The other leader of the centre was Giuseppe Montesano, a psychologist, pioneer of child neuropsychiatry, and founder of the National League for the Protection of Mentally Deficient Children. The two of them, Giuseppe and Maria, were not married but were maintaining a relationship, far from common in their place and time, because nothing about Maria Montessori was ordinary.

When Maria learned she had become pregnant as a single woman, the news weighed heavily upon her. She could force a hasty wedding with Giuseppe and devote herself to raising their child, but that would almost certainly mean abandoning her work and her research. Counter to the norms of the time, Maria's mother did not push for a wedding, which would have made her daughter respectable. In fact, while Renilde Stoppani had not received a formal education, she was nevertheless a cultured woman and treated her daughter's successes as a victory by proxy. 'You have done what no other woman has ever done in Italy. You are a scientist, a doctor, you are everything, and now because of a baby you could lose everything,' she wrote to her daughter around that time. It was Renilde who took care of it all, a mother who knew the price her daughter would pay for also becoming a mother. She decided Maria would have the child, and she'd make the baby disappear the moment he was born. They would give the new-born, whom they named Mario, to a family of farmers in the town of Vicovaro, some forty-five kilometres from Rome, a considerable distance, and a woman there would serve as his wet nurse. On Mario's birth certificate, there's an invented last name, 'Pippilli', since Giuseppe didn't recognise his son until seven years later.

In *The Child Is the Teacher*, biographer Cristina De Stefano compares Maria Montessori's situation with that of other women living in the same period, some of them feminists, like her, who had managed to emancipate themselves somewhat but whose children outside marriage became insurmountable obstacles. Anna Kulishova, doctor, anarchist, and one of the founders of the Italian Socialist Party, a Russian Jew who'd had to flee her country, had a daughter, Andreína, with a fellow member of the party, Andrea Costa, and decided to keep her and take care of her alone. After that, she could never again work in a hospital. She had specialised in gynaecology, and although she had made enormous advances in the field – in her doctoral thesis, she discovered the causative agent of puerperal sepsis, which has saved the lives of countless women – she had to work at the margin of the system, which is why she was known in Rome as 'the doctor of the poor'.

But Kulishova had been living outside the norm since her early adulthood. She got married then divorced, and after having her daughter, she became involved with another socialist, Filippo Turati, but never wanted to marry him. That wasn't the model Renilde, nor Maria herself, wanted to follow. Maria had some protofeminist concerns and plans for the progress of the working class, but she lacked any anti-establishment drive. She had no intention of venturing further outside bourgeois expectations than was necessary. In fact, over the course of her life, she surrounded herself with powerful people in every country she visited. Sometimes dangerously powerful.

Faced with this conundrum, an unexpected pregnancy outside

of marriage, she chose, or they chose for her, the option that while not without its challenges, would keep her closest to the path she had charted for herself. She handed the child over and continued with her research, intrigued by the work of Édouard Séguin, the self-taught educationist who'd studied medicine under Itard, educator of the 'wild boy', Victor of Aveyron – on whom François Truffaut would base his film – and who later implemented an entire system for teaching developmentally delayed children through sensory training. Before he died and fell into obscurity, Séguin wrote a manual in which he suggested that his method could in fact be applied to all kinds of children. Maria Montessori grabbed hold of that thread and continued her work with Giuseppe Montesano, without anyone knowing that the two young, idealistic doctors had secretly had a child.

They maintained this precarious arrangement until September 1901, when Giuseppe suddenly recognised his child and gave him his last name. Days later, without a word to the woman who had been his girlfriend, he married someone else, Maria Aprile. Montesano had ceded to the pressures of his family, who wanted a more conventional partnership for him.

Feeling betrayed, Montessori cut off all her collaborations with the man who had been her romantic and research partner. These new circumstances placed her at an even greater remove from the child, since young Mario now officially had a father, but not a mother. From time to time, she took a carriage to Vicovaro with toys for him. She watched him playing with his milk siblings at a distance, not daring to touch him, and then returned to Rome in a worse state than before.

When Mario was seven years old, his father sent him to a school in Castiglion Fiorentino, near Arezzo, more than two hundred kilometres from Rome. For news of him, Maria had to contact a priest who knew the wet nurse from Vicovaro, who occasionally received letters from the child, or ask friends who had a son at the same school. They always told her the boy was healthy and a good student. In letters to his father, Mario would ask about his mother, and would hear back that she was very busy but would certainly one day appear.

During those years, Maria Montessori threw herself into developing her method and founded the first Children's House, as all her schools would be called from then on, where she applied a child-centric philosophy that consisted not of learning through play, as many believe, but of decentring the adult in the classroom. Although she retained traces of her early socialism, Maria felt more and more Catholic. She had an exhilarating spiritual life and saw the young disciples she was gaining, young apprentices who wanted to be just like her, as part of a kind of secular congregation.

On Christmas Eve in 1910, Maria and some of her followers took vows before an altar. When one of them, Anna Maria Maccheroni, had her ovaries removed and became sterile, Montessori considered it a divine sign. 'Those who devote themselves to my endeavour have to leave all others, sacrifice themselves, and follow me,' she would tell the vestals who lived alongside her, in the imitation feminist commune that wasn't at all erotic. In a way, she was asking them to do as she had to: renounce the children which, in the case of the disciples, were hypothetical, though her own child was very real.

'Many of those who haven't understood me believe I'm a sentimentalist, a romantic, who dreams only of seeing the children, kissing them, telling them fairy tales, and who has to visit all the schools in order to contemplate them, spoil them, and give them candy. Generally, they weary me! I am a rigorous scientific observer, not a literary idealist like Rousseau, and I try to discover the man in the child, to see in him the true spirit of the man, the design of the Creator: the scientific and religious truth.' Montessori never tired of making clear that she was not a universal mother, a foster parent moved only by her love of childhood, but a researcher and scientist in search of a formula. In this case, a method that would serve to educate any child in the world as successfully as possible, drawing out his best and respecting his individuality.

While she was writing all this, she continued to theorise about the emancipation of women and the need to socialise a 'maternal function' with her unusual and very Italian blend of faith, science, and politics. She wanted workers to be able to leave their children at school like the rich, knowing they would have a teacher and a nurse there.

During all those fruitful and busy years, Montessori was weighed down by the constant guilt of being apart from her secret son, whom she not only couldn't see, but whom she couldn't discuss with anyone, not even her own mother. Renilde never wanted to meet her grandson, nor even see him from afar, as Maria occasionally had. Maria had to wait until her mother died, which happened in 1912, to try and salvage the situation.

Without Renilde's breath down her neck, Montessori finally dared to get Mario back, and she did so in the most efficient way. When he was fifteen years old, she wrote him a letter, and he replied that he had been waiting for this moment his whole life and felt no ill will towards her. Shortly after, Maria organised what was in practice a kind of kidnapping, since at that time she had no legal authority over the child. She took advantage of his school's field trip to Arezzo, arrived there herself, then drove off to Rome with him in the car of a friend and patron. His father, who had never got as far as living with their son, accepted this as a fait accompli. From that point on, his mother focused on pouring all her energy into Mario. She called him 'God's masterpiece', 'minnow', 'treasure', and her 'only love'. She wrote in her letters that he was loving, wise, generous, strong, kind, passionate. Although she would continue to attract a court of young women who crowded around her, Maria put aside the idea of the lay congregation of Montessorian teachers organised into small communities, and concentrated on solidifying the pedagogic and economic inheritance she hoped to leave behind for her son. She wrote in her diary, 'Here lies the child's future. Make him secure in his future! Happy – full of compensations for what he suffered: and be I alone that gives him everything.' Wherever they went, she introduced him as her nephew.

After reuniting, mother and son did everything together. Mario belonged to that lineage of sons of great figures, like Dmitri Nabokov or Christopher Tolkien, who dedicate their lives to perfecting and sanctifying the legacies of their fathers, except he did it for his mother, which almost never happens. This makes Mario Montessori a very particular character: not the Master's son, but the Mistress's.

Several of Maria's biographers suggest that it was she – who everyone agrees was extraordinarily resolved, even god-like – who chose her son's first wife. In the midst of World War I, Maria wanted Mario to live in Spain at first, to avoid being conscripted, since the country was often neutral. Barcelona was home to an important Montessorian focal point, looked after by one of Maria's first disciples, funded by the local government, and much more inclined to Catholic spirituality than international Montessorianism generally was. Later, she decided they would relocate to California, where for decades many schools had also been applying her method. There, Mario, who was only nineteen, met an American named Helen Christy. Although her family didn't approve, Maria gave her blessing for a swift wedding and sent the couple on a honeymoon through South America for the duration of the war. By that time, the sale of Montessori materials, which were expensive even then and for which she received a 20 per cent royalty, allowed the family to live comfortably.

Four children were born to Mario and Helen: Marilena, Mario, Rolando, and Renilde. Maria called them her 'Montessori babes'. Marilena explained as an adult that to them, she was not a regular grandmother but a totem, a shining nucleus, the beginning and the end of all that happened in that family.

Mario is credited with initiating the contact that darkens the Montessori name each time his mother comes up, or at least each time she comes up outside of Montessorian hagiography, which is quite extensive. In 1922, the entire family moved from Barcelona, where the children had been born, to Rome, and it was the son – unofficial prime minister of the Montessori empire – who approached Benito Mussolini, to ask that the country that had witnessed the birth of the method, now renowned all over the world, would again begin to seriously support it. The dictator, who had been a teacher when he was young, was enthused by the idea of filling Italy with hard-working Montessorian children and personally assumed the task of imposing the system, which didn't accept half measures (you can't teach in a style that's 'a little Montessori', it has to be all or nothing), on every school in the country, to the resistance of many Italian educators. After a time, Mussolini lost interest in the project, but the bond between the pedagogical movement and fascism was very real. There are letters in which Maria called il Duce the saviour of the human race. She also agreed that a course on fascist culture should be taught in schools that imparted her method, and one instructor who criticised Mussolini was immediately condemned and relieved of her duties. In one of her letters to a Mussolini official, Montessori promised: 'In sum, my method can collaborate with fascism so that it will realise the possibilities to construct great spiritual energies; create a real mental hygiene that, when applied to our race, can enhance its enormous powers that – I am certain – outstrip the powers of all the other races.'

As an elderly woman, Maria also sought out a second wife for her son, who had divorced Helen. She married him to one of her disciples, a Dutch teacher named Ada who was not much older than her eldest grandchild, and who had her full blessing.

Montessori spent her final years living the same itinerant life she had embarked on as an adult, docking in Holland, England, India, collecting honours in France, Scotland, sometimes even Italy. She was a candidate for the Nobel Peace Prize three times but never won, surely because of her murky association with fascism. Before she died in 1952, she named her son ambassador of her entire body of work, and he survived her by thirty years, all of which he spent proselytising the Montessori method.

The love between mother and son, his daughter Marilena said, encompassed everything, ruled his entire existence. Which, seen from a distance, seems oppressive and even toxic. A bubble like the one Maria and her own mother had made for themselves, which left no room for anyone else. It's a striking case of over-compensation following a child's abandonment in infancy. Once she had recovered him, Maria wanted to give him everything: travels, luxuries, a Lancia Lambda he could drive all over Rome, a wife, a career, another wife, a mission, an empire. And Mario accepted it all exactly as he received it, apparently content to live out the stereotype of the child who spends his life latched to his mother's breast, the child who never grows up. Who knows if he was simply trying to erase his fifteen years as a disowned son.

Mercè Rodoreda: Forest Bird

I am an admirer not just of Mercè Rodoreda's books, but also of her presence. The idea of her, that she exists. And that she exists in a time so close to ours, and also in Catalan literature, which is served well by a figure like her: someone unmistakeable, with a healthy accompaniment of drama. If you look closely, Catalan literature has no shortage of drama – how many minor languages have, in their pantheon of illustrious poets, someone like Jacint Verdaguer, an exorcist priest and almost cult figure, a pop idol for the masses?

Still, Rodoreda is on another level. When she died in 1983, her body of work was already considered classic. Her most well-known novel, *In Diamond Square*, had been adapted for film and released just a year before. Rodoreda herself attended the premier, in one of her characteristic minks, with that cloud of white hair she seemed to have had since she was born – the coat and the hair, the keys to Rodoreda's iconicity, what eyeliner and a cigarette were for Clarice Lispector.

At that time, not one student in Catalonia graduated from high school without reading at least one of her books. Usually *In Diamond Square*, but sometimes *Aloma*, her coming-of-age novel, which is short, or *A Broken Mirror*, which worked especially well in a class I took during my third year of secondary school, which was comprised of twenty-eight girls and two boys. For several weeks, in that hyper-hormonal hotbed, we discussed the incest and misfortunes of Teresa Goday and the Valldaura family with an outrage and morbid pleasure we usually saved for school gossip.

Towards the end of her life, Rodoreda finally had money and made herself a home with a garden – the garden she'd lost in her childhood, in Romanyà de la Selva. That woman, who'd had bitter love affairs and gone hungry living in exile, let herself be loved by the relatively new Catalan media, and also, later on, the Madrid media. She appeared on TV and in magazines, and everywhere she went, she casually dropped legendary phrases. She had no interest in fitting in, but she was certainly interested in grandeur. 'I'm insufferable, but my books are not,' she said in an interview. To the author Rosa Chacel, whom she corresponded with and admired, she wrote: 'If you've heard someone speak highly of me as a person, that was an error on the part of whoever was speaking. If goodness is harmony and evil is chaos, I'm an absolutely evil person, because of the chaos I've brought about in my long and already decadent life.'

What had Mercè Rodoreda done to feel so evil? Probably she was referring to her difficult relationships, a complicated life that earned her some enemies. My own biased reading, which connects the Catalan writer with other authors who have shown up in these pages, points to her failed relationship with Jordi, her only son.

In 1939, with the fascist insurrection complete, Rodoreda went into exile, leaving behind a child, then nine years old, in Barcelona. Mostly due to economic hardship and the way their lives evolved, mother and son would never again live under the same roof, and when Jordi was an adult, their relationship definitively ruptured because of an inheritance. They stopped speaking. He was diagnosed with schizophrenia in middle age, when he already had four teenage children. He spent the last decades of his life in a psychiatric hospital, which he only left to be transferred to a care home for the elderly.

The parallels in the lives of Muriel Spark and Mercè Rodoreda are surprising. Two extremely gifted writers of improbable success, two wars, two only sons, two disputed inheritances, two cut threads. And also tranquil twilight years, savouring success, both of them in another woman's company.

When Rodoreda died, pomp was important. There was an improvised lying-in-repose in Girona. Cameras recorded the funeral. The obituaries were long and, up to a point, neutral, as they generally were in the Catalan and Spanish press until recently. Those texts exasperated me. As a nosy reader, interested in the sticky side of life, I get annoyed – and I think this is generational, a reaction I share with my peers – coming up against those articles that, wrapped in respect and grasping at a supposed intellectual loftiness – 'we don't talk about those things here' – almost fall into professional negligence: they paint such partial portraits of the deceased that it's impossible to learn anything about their lives, what broke them, what shook them to their core. There are some shining examples of this genre, which I privately call the 'tidy obituary', and which, luckily, is on its way out as a style. For example, those written for psychiatrist and writer Carlos Castilla del Pino, who lived through the deaths of five of his seven children. Yes, it's true that Castilla del Pino himself, a man as brilliant as he was loathsome, had minimised the impact these deaths had on him in some very high-profile, controversial interviews. But reading articles that condense those five tragedies, each with its own cause and circumstance, into a single paragraph – a single sentence! – like someone talking about moving house, verges on sociopathic. No one wins with a tidy biography.

So what was written about the great writer was excessively serious. But below it, people talked. They talked a lot. About whether Rodoreda had been, in her final years, a member of the Rosicrucian Order, a Christian sect sometimes confused with masonry – she wasn't, although that world had interested her – and about the exact nature of her relationship with Carme Manrubia, the woman she lived with for four years in Romanyà de la Selva, in the last chapter of her life, and who paid the fees at the Muñoz de Girona clinic when the writer was admitted with cancer and close to death. It was Manrubia who was so involved in the Rosicrucian sect, to the point of ensuring that in her villa in El Senyal, where they both spent quite a bit of time, there was a kind of sanctum, a room for Rosicrucian initiation meetings.

Rodoreda and Manrubia met in the thirties while working for the leftist local government and lost track of each other in exile. Manrubia, who was Andalucian, spent hers in Venezuela, where she earned good money selling perfume, and they reunited when older, in Catalonia. The philologist Mariàngela Vilallonga, such an expert in Rodoreda that she has become her digital medium – she maintains the successful Twitter account that carries the writer's name – met Mercè Rodoreda and Carmen Manrubia at the same time. They called her 'the little girl', and in fact, in 1984, Vilallonga ended up buying Carmen Manrubia's house in Romanyà and lived there for many years with her family. As she understood it, the relationship between the two was a platonic infatuation, especially on the part of Manrubia, whom she described as 'very possessive'. To Vilallonga, Manrubia was one of Rodoreda's great mentors, the latest to arrive but nevertheless a great influence on her last works.

When both are mentioned in writing, they're often classified neutrally as 'friends', and it will probably never be clear to what degree that is a euphemism. Even now, there's a reticence when it comes to speaking about the sapphic relationships of many authors, especially in Spain, where the twentieth century was full of closeted and semi-closeted writers, some of whom were enjoying a quiet but very fruitful sort of tutelage. What we do know is that their relationship cooled off in their final years, but Manrubia was at the clinic in Girona when Rodoreda died, and the two are buried in the small cemetery in Romanyà, not beside each other, but one in front of the other.

The second big taboo surrounding the writer and national symbol was her only son, Jordi. So he could attend his mother's funeral, which was full of writers and politicians, they took him out of the psychiatric hospital where he'd been confined for years. Jordi had the disoriented air of those who are heavily medicated. In the middle of the funeral mass, he went up to the altar and yelled: 'I'm Mercè's son, I'm Mercè's son', until someone in the family guided him down and sat him back in his pew.

He was not seen again in public until 2004, when he appeared, at that point quite old, on the programme *El Meu Avi* (*My Grandfather*) on Catalan public television. Putting him in front of the camera was a very deliberate act on the part of the family, who sought, in doing so, to show that Rodoreda had descendants and that they were not ashamed of this unwell man. 'I think it's barbaric to keep him hidden' – said his son Josep Maria, one of Mercè's four grandchildren, on the show – 'I'm proud of my grandmother and my father, even though they say it could hurt my grandmother's image to show her son.'

Nevertheless, in all the extensive biographical writing on Rodoreda, Jordi remains semi-hidden, if not directly ignored.

There are entire books about Rodoreda that barely mention him. They reduce him to a solitary number in the index, a note of little significance. I'm tempted to consider this an anomalous triumph of feminism: here's a woman, Mercè Rodoreda, who has not been defined by family, an author whose role as a mother has mattered as little to those who study her as the role of the father usually does to biographers of male writers. Either that, or it's pure apathy. It's also true there's little to grasp. The letters between mother and son weren't published until 2017, and they aren't especially clarifying. And it didn't occur to anyone to interview Jordi Gurguí before his illness overwhelmed him.

Tant de bo es morís. 'I wish he would die.' Among the very little we know Mercè Rodoreda said about her son, is this chilling phrase. Actually, we can't be sure she said it. We have to trust her good friend Anna Murià, who relayed it. In the prologue of the book that collects their letters, *Cartes a l'Anna Murià (1939–1956)*, she describes the moment when Mercè became a mother as follows: 'She told me herself that her son's arrival had not inspired any tender emotion, but rather resistance, displeasure, rejection. She even told me she had gone as far as thinking: "I wish he would die."'

It's fair to wonder why she said this, if indeed she did. The writer had the child nine months and nineteen days after she married, and the father was her uncle, her mother's brother. It's not hard to imagine Rodoreda, age twenty, with barely any friends outside her family circle, experiencing that pregnancy with terror, authentic disgust, because it came out of a union so close to incest it had even required a papal bull.

Up to that point, Rodoreda had lived her life like a flower in a greenhouse. Born in 1908 in a home in Sant Gervasi, which at that point was its own town, separate from Barcelona, she would spend the rest of her life constructing an entire personal mythology around that idyllic, cosy childhood. In 1973, she described it as follows to the writer Montserrat Roig for the magazine *Serra D'Or*:

> My family belonged to the petite bourgeoisie. At home, there were two terrific people: my mother and my grandfather. My father was a bookkeeper on Calle Ferran, and was what we now call that very ugly word: *letraherida* [letterstruck]. He read out loud to me when I was a child, and put the Catalan language in my head and in my heart.

The beloved grandfather, who had been an antiques dealer, hung old plates on the façade of the family house, the famous *torre* – in Catalonia, any single-family home of considerable size is called a tower – and when it was windy, everything clattered and jingled.

When Grandfather Pere suffered a stroke, Mercè's mother took her out of school, and she returned only sporadically, stopping entirely at age twelve. She always envied students and felt a certain shame around her education, so chaotic and informal, though profound. Young Mercè was constantly reading the Catalan classics, but also everything else, old and new. She adored Virginia Woolf. She read Proust and Joyce. With Katherine Mansfield, she felt that very specific envy good writers feel towards other good writers, living or dead, when they read sentences they would give their right arm for.

Her connection with the literary world began at an early age, and she wanted to be a journalist. She went to see the director of the magazine *La Rambla*, who told the young girl from Sant Gervasi, more than a little condescendingly: 'First live, and then write.' She ignored him because she was too bored; she wrote because she was bored.

And then that doomed marriage. Again, Rodoreda mirrors Spark. Did they both get married so young, to much older men whom they clearly didn't love, for the same reason people do so many things, to do *something*, to introduce a narrative twist into the monotony of their lives?

Joan Gurguí, Rodoreda's future husband, had emigrated to Buenos Aires when he was essentially still a child. According to family lore, they sent him with thirteen pesetas, a rucksack containing some cheese, and a letter to introduce him to one of his father's friends, a baker who, as it turned out, had been dead for years. The new bakery owner took care of the Catalan boy and gave him work making deliveries. The stories of Spanish immigrants who became rich in Latin America are often told as rags-to-riches tales, sparing any details that might detract from the narrative arc: in a few years, Joan, who had a good head for numbers, made a fortune in the real estate sector, and he returned to Barcelona, triumphant, in 1921. His niece, Mercè, the only daughter of his sister Montserrat, was thirteen.

Joan Gurguí's American money elevated the profile of the whole family, which up until that point had been modestly middle class. When the American uncle returned, he introduced order, a kind of formality, but also – inside the home – something somewhat sinister. For Mercè, the arrival of her uncle marked the end of her childhood. From one day to the next, she went from being the little girl of the house, to a future bride.

There are those who maintain that the wedding between uncle and niece was contrived by Mercè's mother with the sole objective of keeping the money he had made in Argentina in the family. Mercè's daughter-in-law, Margarida Puig, always defended that theory, which some biographers dispute, since the writer never seemed to harbour any resentment towards her mother, and some bitterness would have been expected if Montserrat was to blame for her absurd wedding. In the letters she wrote from exile, there's a genuine concern for her mother that lasts until the end of her days.

In 1924, when Rodoreda was sixteen years old and three years had passed since her uncle had returned from Argentina, the plan was already in motion and seemed almost inevitable. The author wrote in her diary: 'I remember that when I didn't want to, when I told him yes, I would marry him, he hugged me very tightly and, kissing me, said: you'll be my life, if you love me, everything I have will be for you, money, everything, I won't deny you anything you ask for.' Shortly after, she also wrote of her uncle: 'What a bad personality he has! I don't know if we get along. His temper really scares me, [. . .] he's too much of a tyrant, and he only wants done what he orders.'

Nothing impeded the wedding. No one thought better of it. No other suitor crossed paths with Mercè, nor did Joan find another match. And on 10 October 1928, uncle and niece were married in the Bonanova church in upper Barcelona. The reception took place in the same family home where Mercè had been born and raised. The groom was thirty-four, the bride turned twenty that day. The papers had arrived from Rome on time, the papal bull that made possible a Catholic wedding between blood relatives.

The entire family left the tower and moved into a more comfortable home, number 16 on Calle Zaragoza. The bride and groom went on honeymoon in Paris, and there, Mercè quickly learned that she couldn't count on the uncle-husband even when it came to leading the carefree life she had dreamed of. She told her friends that, in a shop on Saint-Honoré, where

Mercè was trying on minks, Joan threw himself to the floor to beg for a discount.

Nine months and nineteen days after the wedding, in July 1929, Jordi was born, the 'unwanted son', according to Anna Murià: *Tant de bo es morís*, I wish he would die.

In 1985, Murià was asked in an interview, also printed in the book that gathered their correspondence, how it was that her friend spoke so little about her child. She responded with: 'Her son's birth didn't excite her, it bothered her. When she had him, she was very young [. . .]. She got married too young, and then she had a child right away, and at that age, he was a bother. Afterwards, of course, maybe a child, when you live with him, endears you to him.' On one occasion, Mercè did say in a letter that she, Anna, was lucky to have had a child with a man she loved. Maybe Rodoreda was experiencing something along the lines of what Muriel Spark had, looking at her male son and seeing nothing in his small face but the face of her husband. Maybe it was too hard to separate the children from their fathers, and from the unhappy, claustrophobic marriages that had produced them.

It's hard to imagine what Rodoreda's first nine years as a mother were like. She spent them locked up like some pre-war Rapunzel, surrounded by all the same family as before, except now, her uncle was also her husband, his power over her doubled. Mercè was obsessed with the idea of earning money of her own, seeking some economic freedom. She achieved this in part by working for the Generalitat Ministry of Culture, as the charge of another writer, Joan Oliver. She wrote every day. She enrolled at the Liceu Dalmau to try and fill the holes in her education. She published stories in magazines like *Clarisme*, and also wrote plays. All that literary activity, which we might call a kind of warm-up, had two crucial outcomes: it made her realise that writing was what mattered to her most, and it significantly widened her circle, which up until that point had been suffocatingly small. She joined a group called the Club dels Novel·listes, the objective of which was to 'promote the novel as the central axis of a modern literature'.

The eruption of the Spanish Civil War coincided, for Rodoreda, with the final disintegration of her marriage. It was the Club dels Novel·listes that led to her meeting another key figure in the story, the politician and trade unionist Andreu Nin, who also had a double life as an intellectual. Nin was responsible for translating great Russian literature into Catalan (*Crime and Punishment, Anna Karenina*, some Chekhov) and he did that while also founding the Partido Obrero de Unificación Marxista, the Workers' Party of Marxist Unification – a crucial player in the Spanish Civil War – and advocating for international unionism.

In her biography of Mercè Rodoreda, Marta Pesarrodona writes that there is evidence the two of them were acquainted as early as 1935. Nin, who witnessed the Russian Revolution, returned to Catalonia in 1930, with a Russian wife and two children. And in 1935, Rodoreda published a children's story in the magazine *La Publicitat*, titled 'La noieta daurada' ('The Golden Lass'), dedicated specifically to Ira, one of Nin's daughters. Again, the principal witness to this affair, of which there is little evidence, is Anna Murià. According to her, it was 'the most intense and secret drama of Mercè Rodoreda's existence in 1937'. Murià also says that their love remained unconsummated: 'They had no time, they killed him.' Nin was disappeared in June of that year as part of a Marxist purge. The historian Paul Preston maintains that he was tortured to death, skinned alive.

Consummated or not, her connection to Andreu Nin was enough to end things with Gurguí. When he simply couldn't believe that there was no sexual relationship between Mercè and the revolutionary, she showed him her only letter from Nin as proof. He tore it to bits, and she gathered them up and kept them. For two years (two years of war and the start of exile), Rodoreda carried around the pieces of the letter from Andreu Nin. 'I travel the world with a letter torn to shreds,' Murià recalls her friend telling her. Gurguí apparently begged his wife for days not to go. He cried, he kissed her feet (like Eladi kisses Sofia's in one of her best novels, *A Broken Mirror*). Also around that time, Rodoreda may have had another relationship with her colleague from the Club dels Novel·listes and the Generalitat, the writer Francesc Trabal, with whom she shared a work trip to Prague.

Her husband's pleas were unsuccessful. In mid-1937, Rodoreda took Jordi and left the marital home to go and live with her parents. They never got as far as an official divorce, but from that point on, the writer was, in effect, a separated woman. Again, like Muriel Spark: a woman alone with her son, in the middle of a war.

At the beginning of January 1939, the arrival of Franco's troops to Barcelona felt imminent, and took place on the 26th of that month. All those who knew to expect repercussions if they remained tried desperately to cross the border to France. The Ministry of Culture made an evacuation plan for Catalan writers. They put them in a bibliobus, one of those buses that were used to take books to the front, and sent them off to the border with a collective passport. Rodoreda had not been highly politically active, but she was a member of the Unión General de Trabajadores, the General Union of Workers, like all her writer friends, and she was indisputably engaged with Catalanism.

Leaving was the safest thing to do. Could she have taken Jordi, who was nine at the time, along with her? Some writers who left in the bibliobuses took their families with them. It seems Rodoreda didn't consider it. Many years later, in 1985, Anna Murià was asked directly: did the writer make any attempt to bring her son to France? She responded, 'No. Nothing. She calmly left him with her mother. We had no idea the thing would last for so many years, we thought it would be brief, we knew nothing, we fled without knowing what was in store for us.'

At that point, Rodoreda already had many enemies in the Catalan literary world. She had a reputation for being frivolous and adulterous. The more famous she became later – the more obvious her talent – the more her rivals resented her. Some of them have written about her. Like Carola Fabra, daughter of the linguist considered the father of modern Catalan, Pompeu Fabra, who said that Mercè took her father's seat on the bus and was laughing 'like we were on a bender'.

The first months of exile, when the writers were based in a chateau in Roissy-en-Brie, could have been, and certainly were, full of pain and uncertainty, but for Mercè and for Anna, they were also their most exciting days, a compacted youth, a spring-like vaudeville of romantic intrigue. The different authors who were there have used terms like 'erotic atmosphere' and 'ambiguous paradise' in reference to those days.

Much has been written about the erotic qualities of war, and that group of young writers and their partners had just lost one and were already sensing the next. At Roissy, Rodoreda began what would be the most significant romantic relationship of her life, with another writer, Joan Prat i Esteve, better known as Armand Obiols. In her letters to Anna Murià, she sometimes refers to him as 'Monsieur de Madame per una estona', temporary

Mister to the Missus. Obiols was also married to Montserrat Trabal, the sister of Francesc, who was in Roissy as well and was, let's not forget, Rodoreda's ex-lover. The world of Catalan letters was very conducive to this kind of inbreeding and entanglement. Obiols' wife had stayed behind in Sabadell with their new-born daughter.

The nascent union between the two muddied that of the whole group, which was divided between those who sided with Mercè, the lover, and those who sided with Montserrat, the wife. So much so that some wouldn't let Mercè sit at the table at mealtimes, and the group had to split up. The writer started her long exile with a scarlet letter, which amused her more than it bothered her at that point.

The relationship between Rodoreda and Obiols persisted for decades with varying intensities, until Obiols died in Vienna in 1971. Both had experienced financial hardship – for years, Rodoreda took sewing jobs – and real danger during the Nazi occupation of France, when Obiols was captured and sent to the Lindemann concentration camp, although his time there and his subsequent engagements with agencies like the International Labour Organization and UNESCO are shadowy. Suspicions that he collaborated with the Germans hang over him. Obiols also never reunited with his family. His wife and daughter went to Chile, like so many others from Catalonia, although later, in 1948. In 1971, when Obiols was already very sick in Vienna, Rodoreda visited him and found another woman at the head of the bed. It was a hard jolt, even for Mercè, who was used to receiving them.

And Jordi? He remains notoriously absent from the enormous quantity of literature *about* Rodoreda, and even literature *written by* Rodoreda. There's no trace of the letters he wrote to his mother, but there are some that she wrote to him from exile.

They're included in the volume *Cartes de guerra i d'exili*, complied in 2017 by Carme Arnau. The letters are pragmatic. Every single one of them talks about money: how much Mercè has sent to the grandmother, how much the son has asked his father for but not received, how much they need to be able to travel and see each other, how much to start a business. Many of them also talk about *turrón*, the classic Spanish nougat confection. Jordi and his grandmother sent some to Mercè every Christmas, to Paris or Geneva or wherever she happened to be, and often they were lost in the post, or took forever to arrive. Reading the letters, one can sense a mild love between mother and son, an affection without outbursts or reproaches, at least not explicit ones. In the earliest one that remains, from 1948, they hadn't seen each other for a decade, since before she left for exile. Mercè says she thinks it wise that he focus on business rather than study for a degree, to minimise any hardship: 'You're one of the boys (and there are hundreds, if not thousands) who have been a little shattered by the war.' Then she talks about the parties she's going to throw and half promises they'll dance together.

The most frequently referenced moment in their letters is one in which the mother defines herself as an '*ocellot de bosc*', a big forest bird, and says that her son, on the other hand, is a 'caged canary'. Birds are a recurring motif: in other letters, Rodoreda even draws a small winged creature. It's understood that the mother wishes her son were a little less meek, a little more adventurous. She encourages him to have fun, to be impulsive. Maybe, although she doesn't say so, she was disappointed he married so young, that he rushed to form such a conventional family.

Outside of the letters, to learn more about the relationship between Mercè and Jordi, one must rely on Margarida, Jordi's wife. In 2016, already advanced in years, Margarida Puig wrote some pages she appropriately titled *The Last Word*. With no literary ambitions, but in a style that illuminates all the peculiarities of her time and her class, Puig explains the entire story of her marriage, and her relationship with her unique mother-in-law.

Margarida and Jordi met in 1953, on a kind of blind date set up by her aunt and his grandmother. She earned money as a piano teacher, he was working as a salesperson. They had a chaste and supervised courtship in a provincial Barcelona reminiscent of the one Carmen Laforet describes in *Nada*.

According to Margarida, Jordi felt more resentment towards his father than his mother. She recounts how he recalled fleeing the family home at age four, after his parents fought about the famous letter – it's impossible to be sure if Jordi knew the letter's author was the renowned murdered leftist. She also says that his grandmother, who was at the same time his aunt, had forced that marriage.

After the war, the child was sent to boarding school, first with the Salesians, then the Jesuits. The family found the means to stitch together an acceptably bourgeois education for him. One must also imagine that, growing up in a boarding school, the boy had to absorb a double separation, first from his mother, and then from his grandmother, who had raised him.

Even so, Jordi always expressed admiration for his absent mother, so much so that his bride, Margarida, began to feel some hostility towards the woman. 'My mother writes novels', or 'my mother lives in Paris', he constantly told her. One day the famous *mamà* appeared – that's what Jordi always called his mother, a formulation he considered more distinguished than the *mare* of the working-class families.

So Margarida met her illustrious mother-in-law, who by that point had been crossing the border for years to sporadically visit the family. On that occasion, she made the trip to meet her son's fiancée. The encounter was brief, cordial but cloaked in formality. Margarida understood, and says in her writing, that her relationship with her mother-in-law would be 'political, maybe. Or should I say, diplomatic.' The couple married and had four children. There are photos of Rodoreda at one of her grandchildren's baptisms. 'Mercè really liked to be the eccentric grandmother, like in Agatha Christie,' writes the daughter-in-law. She liked to show up unannounced. She offered the eldest, also named Jordi, his first cigar. The second eldest, she gave a bicycle. These were the years when Rodoreda was finally starting to make money from her writing and could spend it however she liked, making up for thirty years of privations.

Jordi was working in hardware distribution. It seems he didn't share the reading achievements or preoccupations of his mother, who hadn't had the time or space to pass them on. The *letraherida* – that term Rodoreda hated – line of the Gurguí family ended with her. The family moved to another tower, in Bonanova. When Mercè went to visit, she stayed at a hotel. They lived the conventional life of an upper-middle-class Catalan family, as Margarida herself describes, citing Christian and pagan rites: 'Saint days, birthdays, blessing the palmones [on Easter], Christmases'.

Grandmother Montserrat died first, and then, in 1971, his father, Joan, the man who cried at Mercè Rodoreda's feet. That's when everything broke down between mother and son, because of a very Rodoredan element: a will. Joan had left in writing that everything that belonged to him was to go to his son, on one condition: he couldn't sell any of it until Mercè died. He gave her the jewellery, which she had returned to him the day she left home with young Jordi, and since they had never divorced, she was still entitled to her share, the so-called 'marital quarter', an amount guaranteed, at that time, to go to the wife, but she demanded that her son give up a larger portion. He refused, saying he had four children to feed. They argued all night, then she left, and they never spoke again.

In her writing, Margarida is strangely oblique when it comes to what she calls the 'behaviour' of her husband. 'He started to change,' she writes, but she doesn't explain how or into what; we don't know what this hardware salesman, father of four, started to do that led to his schizophrenia diagnosis. The next thing his wife describes is that, 'pressured by the doctors', she was forced to admit him to the psychiatric hospital Pere Mata, in the town of Reus. It's not surprising that a woman of her generation would express anything related to mental health with those ellipses and that primness, but it's very difficult to understand what was going on in the mind of Jordi Gurguí, and if any of these problems had manifested before. Margarida sent two telegrams to her mother-in-law in Geneva about his admission. According to her, she received no response.

The two women saw each other only once more. The eldest grandchild, Jordi, was going to be married, and he saw on TV that his famous grandmother Mercè was in Barcelona. He wanted to invite her, and his mother, Margarida, paid a visit to her mother-in-law in the house she had bought at the top of Calle Balmes. Mercè told her she couldn't attend the wedding, that she had a 'very well paid' interview – which seems strange, since interviews are usually unpaid – with Swiss TV. They tiptoed around the matter of the son, still in the sanitorium. 'These things with the nerves can go on a while, but he'll get better, you'll see,' was all Mercè Rodoreda had to say.

They took Jordi out of the hospital to go to his mother's funeral. 'Of that day, I'll never forget the figure of Mercè Rodoreda's son' – writes Puig, referring to her own husband, the father of her children, with that curious periphrasis – 'Aged, sick, without any idea what was happening around him, looking at the body of his mother. He gestured to her with his hand and said simply, "My mother". And what could I say except "Yes, Jordi". There are no words. I didn't know how to find them.'

In Mercè Rodoreda's books, motherhood always has a murky, if not sinister, component. Her most famous creation, the protagonist of *In Diamond Square*, is Natàlia, Colometa, or 'little dove', as her husband has christened her. Here is another woman forced into becoming a baby animal, like Ibsen's Nora. Natàlia grows up without her mother. When she herself becomes pregnant, she detests it, just as she detests sex with her husband, which she finds painful. Natàlia's two pregnancies in *In Diamond Square* are two of the most anguished in modern literature. She experiences them as invasions that make her a stranger in her own body. This is how she describes being pregnant with her first son, Toni: 'My hands swelled, my ankles swelled, and if they'd roped me to my bed, one push would have been enough to float me [. . .] I felt as if I'd been drained empty again and was being pumped back up by something very peculiar.' After the birth, which is painful and exhausting, Natàlia doesn't have enough milk to nurse the child. Her friend Julieta tells her the boy is going die, 'because if a baby refused to suckle, it was as good as dead already'. When she gives birth to her second child, a daughter named Rita, Natàlia loses so much blood she almost dies.

Later, when the war is escalating, and her husband, Quimet, is on the front, Colometa has no choice but to become an abandoner. For a time, she sends her elder child, Antoni, to one of the camps for refugee children where Julieta works, though he doesn't want to go. Was Rodoreda, older at this point, thinking about her son, Jordi, when she wrote this? In her many letters – it's funny to note that Rodoreda is sparing with her style in most of them, conserving her best resources for the ones to her writer friends, whom she wants to seduce with her prose – Rodoreda never gives the impression that she's tormented by being so far away from her son. Yes, by her lack of money, or by her anomalous situation with Armand Obiols, or a literary life that slips by as she sews dressing gowns, but not especially over a child who she knows is well looked after in another city, with whom she exchanges pleasant letters. Still, who can presume to know anything about anyone. Not even her friend Anna Murià, not even her readers.

The war Natàlia lives through is worse than her author's. When the fighting is over, Colometa can't find work because she's married to a leftist, and she's hungry all the time. That's when she makes the decision that marks the cruellest point in the novel. Since she cannot feed her two children, she decides to kill them. Twice, she goes to the chemist to buy hydrochloric acid and a funnel. The plan is to poison the children first, then kill herself the same way. The first time she goes, she isn't able to do it, she doesn't buy the poison because she changes her mind. But she goes back. The second time, the owner offers her work. This is as close as *In Diamond Square* gets to a fairy tale, especially because fifteen months later, they marry. There's a bonus for Natàlia, one that definitively cancels out any romantic or conventional aspect to *In Diamond Square*. The new husband was made impotent in the war. There will be no more painful penetrations for Natàlia, nor will there be more children. The idea of a stable, safe, and asexual marriage, which cannot end in motherhood, is the closest thing to a happy ending for this woman whom fate has served so poorly.

Jordi Gurguí, the only son of Mercè Rodoreda, died in 2005,

after spending four decades in psychiatric institutions. His wife, Margarida, survived him until 2021. One of their children said in a TV documentary that he didn't blame his grandmother for anything, that it was better she had devoted herself to what she knew how to do, which was write. On that point, I dare say grandson and grandmother would have agreed.

If You Have Children, *Mija*

Usually, if a father isn't raising his child half or even a quarter of the time, it's because he doesn't want to. And if a mother isn't, it's because she can't. What separates mothers from their children all over the world daily is not the difficulty of maintaining a creative or intellectual life, nor the incompatibility of the child with a new romantic relationship, nor even a separation, but money. Money explains 98 per cent of the cases in which a mother has left her child. And up until now, this book been occupied with the other 2 per cent.

Obviously, I'm making up the percentages. No record exists.

The other abandoners, the involuntary ones, are everywhere. Women who go far away and leave their children, almost always in the care of their own mothers, who cross to the other side of the world and devote themselves, often, to caring for others' children. Their stories are barely told, not even in journalism, although they're now beginning to find a place in some books and movies, mostly relayed from the point of view of the Westerners who benefit from their care.

This chapter of *The Abandoners* was always on thin ice. I nearly cut it several times, because it was different. I explained to Anna, my editor, that I didn't want it to be influenced by my white guilt, nor to feel how I did every year when I had to talk to Kevin's mum.

Who is Kevin, Anna asked, what are you talking about? Kevin is the kid who has been tormenting my son since his first year of school. Each finds the other strangely fascinating, maybe because they're nothing alike at all. This fixation, unfortunately, has not blossomed into a lovely friendship that allows them to understand the value in difference, as might happen in a children's film with an inspirational message, but has instead generally been realised in the form of Kevin hitting my son, and me having to call to complain to the school and his family.

Kevin's mother is a single woman who migrated to Barcelona and whose life story has been quite difficult, and each time I have to reach out to her to ask whether it's possible for her son to hit mine less, I'm overwhelmed with white guilt, fully aware of the scene that she and I form in front of the school entrance. I am a middle-class mother, and she is a mother facing economic hardship. Every time it happens, I'm aware that, in that moment, I'm adding one more problem to the many she already has, and what's more, I'm singling out her child as an aggressor, with darker skin and fewer financial resources than my own. In short, I could end myself right there for embodying that horrible stereotype, a Catalan Karen, a liberal mum at a public school in a centrally located neighbourhood where inclusivity is sometimes easier to preach than it is to practise. Then I think about my oldest son, maybe the sweetest boy in the world, and tell myself I have to do it, and I'll probably have to again in a few months' time.

These involuntary abandoners, like Kevin's own mother, who also left a son in her country, deserve much more than one chapter. They deserve two hundred books, preferably written and narrated by them. But whatever this book is, it would not be complete if I didn't include them in it.

So in order to write this chapter, the strange one, the one that doesn't fit, the one that doesn't talk about writers or actors or famous pedagogues, I interviewed migrant women who are living in Spain today, employed in hospitality or domestic work. And what materialised was a catalogue of ruptures, of pieces that don't quite fit. Kids left in their countries of origin, kids born in Europe but sent back by their mothers when they realised it was impossible to spend twelve hours a day doing domestic labour and care for their children at the same time, kids whose mothers were able to bring them to Spain after many years of effort, savings, and paperwork, and who, in some cases, have yet to adapt.

It was clear to me that the mothers with an ocean between them and their children are anything but abandoners. They barely allow themselves to grow their lives here, or have partners, and that's a problem. Often they self-enforce the highest possible degree of maternal sacrifice. They are merciless with themselves and deny themselves any relief, any diversion, that might take place far away from their children, as if to punish themselves. Their minds are always where their children are, and that's also where they send almost all of their earnings, which, it goes without saying, are scarce. With technology now, they are able to be much more connected than they were a few decades ago, but that, in turn, generates new obligations, rituals that aren't always easy. Calling at midnight after working ten hours, when there's nothing left to offer, doing four hours of homework on FaceTime, talking for hours to a child who is on his PlayStation just so his mother's voice won't sound strange to him, saving for years for holidays together that, when they finally come, bring with them the anxiety of knowing they'll soon be over.

These are the stories of some of those women, exactly as they tell them. Their names have been changed to protect their privacy. I'm enormously grateful to them for their trust. Some hesitated at first, but then the words sprang up, unstoppable.

Violet B., Nicaragua, 51 years old

In my country, I worked at a hospital, as a medical secretary. But you don't make much there. One day a friend of mine came to Spain, and she got us excited. She told us to come, that in Spain, you could make more. I was going to come with another friend's sister, but she backed out, and I already had my ticket. I came alone, I didn't know anyone. It was the first time I'd left my country.

I'm separated, *mija*. I had my daughter alone and I've raised her alone. You fight for your kids. When you have kids, you do everything for them. My daughter was sixteen when I came to Spain. She stayed behind with my mum and one of my sisters. For six months, she cried and cried. They took her to a psychologist. Every time we called each other from the internet café, we both cried. Seeing her cry made me emotional. Until one day my sister said: stop, this is just worse. I had to grin and bear it.

My daughter said: 'You left, you abandoned me.' It's hard to hear your daughter say that.

I came with goals, with the purpose of getting ahead. Helping my family, so she could study, build my home in Nicaragua. That's what you come for, at least if you're responsible. Lots of women come and start partying all the time, they think 'What do I have to lose?' They give up everything, even their kids, they leave them to fend for themselves. There are all kinds.

I didn't see my daughter Stephany again until six years later, until I got my papers. Then she was already twenty-two. It was nice, but you miss so many things. She only talked to her grandmother and looked at me like I was a stranger. That really hurt. I was there for just a month, and that was even harder. You see the difference. You lose that familiarity. When they're littler, it's even worse. The kids don't recognise you. It's as if you're just an object that's there.

If you have children, don't leave them, *mija*. It's the saddest thing you can do.

In Spain, I've done everything but sex work. I've taken care of the elderly. I've cleaned houses. Now I work at a nursing home. I've taken care of families with kids. I brought up some twins. It's hard to take care of other people's kids. They pay us to take care of them, feed them, and the love you have, you give it to these other children. Those little twins, their mum handed them right over when they were born, and I took care of them for two years. If you hire someone and you free yourself from your kids, well, the kids stick to whoever's taking care of them. Those kids were so attached to me. I was the one who went and got them at eight in the morning, I put them to bed at night, Monday to Saturday. I bathed them, I fed them, I did everything for them. The little girl was sharp. They said something was off with the boy, but I didn't think so. The mum, she got jealous. She told the boy, when he was four months old: 'Mateo, I'm your mum, not Violet.' They didn't call her mum. They called her 'Bertaaa, Bertaaaa'. The dad told me they would pay me for Sundays too. They couldn't do it alone. The babies never stopped crying with them.

I would talk to them, and the little ones knew my voice. They would calm down. It drove the parents crazy. In the end, the psychologist told the parents they had to separate them from me, that one day, I wouldn't be there. They sent them to nursery school, and when they got home, they shut them up in a room. The kids fought to open the door. I was taking it hard. They were taking it hard. But the mum made sure I stayed away from them. Then the señor told me: 'The psychologist said we had to separate you and the children, we've already put them in day-care, we won't need you anymore.' It took me a month to recover. You give the kids love, care, tenderness. You feed them, you hear their first words, you see them take their first steps. I loved all that.

After the twins, I didn't want to take care of any more kids. I prefer the elderly now.

My Stephany also got jealous when I was working with kids, because even though she's older now, that's how my daughter thinks. She was born with something a little off, and she wasn't like other teenagers. She had a hard time learning. We don't really know what her mental age is.

About two years ago, I brought her to Spain. It was bad. We would walk down the street, *mija*, and she would walk in front and I would walk behind, like a dog. She wasn't comfortable with me. She saw me as a stranger. She didn't have that bond with me a daughter should have. Then one day I got mad because she was being cold to me, and I scolded her. Whatever you think I am, I'm the bitch that gave birth to you. I'm your mother, I told her, don't drag me around like a dog. In the end, she went back. She had a boyfriend there, and his boxers were calling her more than I was, I guess.

I've had no boyfriends here. I don't want any trouble. I want peace. I'm at an age where I've met my goals. I built my little home in my country, they have people renting it. But I've been here for so many years now. Sooner or later, I'll have to leave.

Mija, if you have children, don't you leave them.

Caslissha C., Nicaragua, 36 years old

My husband and I are both engineers, and we were working for the same company. When my country's government started withholding raw material, the company lost money. First they fired me, because I was overseeing one area, and the people in my role made a little more. We were already thinking one of us would have to leave the country. It was a hard decision, but I left, because there are more options for women here, with all the domestic work. When men come, it takes forever for them to find something.

It took me six months to make up my mind. It was a bitter pill to swallow.

I'd been telling my daughter, who was four, that mummy was going to have to leave the country, that we weren't going to be together again for a while. Eventually, I left while she was sleeping. I was unable to say goodbye. Not to my daughter, not to my family, not to anyone. Not even to my grandmother, who was like a mother to me. At the airport, I didn't really say goodbye to my husband either. I just wanted to get to the gate. I had been holding back tears the whole way there, but I didn't cry on the flight. Even today, I still haven't cried. What does crying get you? I feel like I want to, but I can't. Maybe when I get back. It might be that once I'm there, I just break down.

When I got to the airport in Barcelona, the first thing I thought was that I wanted to go back. I thought: 'My God, what am I doing here.' Up to that point, I had only been an hour or two from my city. I came in a plane, that almost killed me.

I talk to my daughter, Yasmine is her name, every day. We share things, we do her schoolwork together. I have her in school in the morning and then two hours with a tutor in the afternoon. I have a WhatsApp chat with the tutor. I bought her a phone, and if it were up to her, we'd talk twenty-four hours a day. We haven't lost that.

When I first got here, my little girl didn't understand. She thought I might appear again at any moment. She thought I was close but just couldn't get there. Now she gets it a little more. I've been here for two years. I told her I would come back, but the elderly man I was caring for died, and I'm out of work. I can't come back without money. Now she says: 'Come back, Daddy can take care of us both.' She's very smart, she understands so much. She's always asking questions. She says when I get back from Spain, she's going to sleep tied to me. I sometimes think when I get back she won't be able to sleep, afraid I'll leave her again in the night.

I've taken care of children here. First a baby, and then a four-year-old. There's no conflict in it for me. It's very clear that one thing is a job, and the other is my daughter. Yes, I care for them, but not how a mother cares. The same way it's my job to love them, but it's not a mother's love. A mother's love is for her daughter.

What I can't do is sit in the park, because then I get nostalgic. But you know, I still don't cry. What good would crying do.

Noemy R., Colombia, 45 years old

I had my daughter very young. My father was pretty sexist, he didn't make us go to school. I worked as a waitress in his restaurant, and I got pregnant at, like, twenty-one or twenty-two. When the girl was born, I gave her to my parents so they could take care of her. Some of my friends were coming to Spain and they told me there was work here, so I came. I could already see the girl was going to need her things, her schooling.

I arrived in Oviedo all alone, I didn't know a single person. It was 1998, and there was no WhatsApp like now, no FaceTime or Skype. We bought little phone cards called Llama Ya and we could connect to Colombia for a few minutes. I called her every day.

I started working with the elderly and with children. That's what I could do, because I didn't have papers. I fell in love and got myself a Spanish boyfriend who promised me heaven and earth, he told me he would marry me and that he would give me everything . . . We went to live in a pueblo in Asturias. But it only lasted five years. Luckily, when I left him, the government was legalising undocumented immigrants. I met a girl who hired me to take care of her grandmother, and that's when I got my papers.

So I could go back to Colombia to see my daughter, who was seven by then. I got there, and she was already a little lady. Smart, really clever. My mum helped out a lot. When she was little, she always said to her: your mum left so you could have all these toys. She sent you this and that.

I brought the girl over when she was twelve or thirteen, but she didn't adapt. In Colombia, she lived in a small city, she connected with her teachers, they cared about her, they took walks with her . . . She would cry here. She was very mature for her age. She felt big compared to the other children. I had two jobs at that point. In the morning, from eight to noon, I cleaned a house and took care of a little girl, and in the evenings, from three to midnight, I was working in a café. We almost never saw each other. My friend went on walks with her, and at night, she came and did her homework at the café. She was very alone. She called my mum in Colombia and told her: I live on the eighth floor, when I go out I don't see anyone. She was used to going out and seeing her friends.

High school was hard for her, the schoolwork. And suddenly she was becoming a woman, bringing boys round. We had to adapt to each other. She was so young when I left Colombia that, while she knew I was her mother, I was basically a stranger. We butted heads a lot, she was very rebellious. Sometimes she would say: 'You're not my mum, you didn't raise me.'

Eventually, I quit my waitressing job because I was having problems with the owner, who was racist and terrible. Just then the Spanish financial crisis started. Some friends told me we could find work in Italy, and I went. I left my daughter in Oviedo, with her boyfriend. She was fifteen and they were already living together. I came and went every three weeks until she told me she wanted to go back to Colombia, with her aunts and her grandmother. I told her OK, and she didn't come back again. It must be because of the lack of a father figure, she's always been big on relationships, having a boyfriend. Now she's living with a boy in Mexico. She's pretty mature for her age, a traveller, like her mother. She's found her footing. We talk on the phone a lot, we'll talk for an hour, like friends. Now I think how I wish I'd had more time for her. She would still be here.

Cristina, Colombia, 37 years old

Soon, it'll be five years since I came to Madrid. In Colombia, I worked in medical services, but the company went bankrupt and shut down. Finding work there is incredibly difficult, so I came here looking for new horizons. My sister was already here and a friend told me: 'Cristina, come to Madrid, there's a lot of work here.' But it wasn't true. When I got here, I was doing a little of everything. Gardening, cleaning, Colombian empanadas . . . until I found something a bit steadier in a café. I sent money to my country religiously, to help my parents out.

My son was four and a half when I came, and now he's nine. I left him with his father, we're separated, and with my parents, who have raised him. I call every day and he tells me things. With the pandemic, they're doing school virtually now. On Mondays, they send us the guides on WhatsApp, and it's like I'm his teacher. Sometimes I'm exhausted, but I feel like he has homework to turn in, and, well, I make an effort. Natural sciences, English, maths, religion, everything. There are days when at two in the morning I'm still doing homework. I call him around ten at night when I'm out of work, which is two in the afternoon there, and we spend hours talking.

Other times he's on his PlayStation and I talk to him. Or he's showering and I talk to him. It gets harder every year, because you feel like you're missing so much.

When I came here, I told him: 'Son, it's for your own well-being,' half-explaining the situation. Apparently, he got it, but sometimes I realise there's something tender there. When we do the homework for ethics and values and things like that, and he has to self-reflect, I see the answers and I understand that things haven't been easy for him. One day he told me, 'I'm a very sad person.' Those days, I want to cry.

Margarita, Peru, 50 years old

I was born in the south of Peru, in Apurímac, in the mountains. My parents had many children, and they were poor, so they gave me to a woman in the city whose kids were already older. In those days, it wasn't unusual to give your kids to another woman. They gave me to her when I was seven. I called her my godmother. There were a few of us, she kept us in her home and treated us like the help. She was never happy with anything. Now that I'm an adult, I see the first thing a child needs is love, hugs, and I never had that. When I think about that, it makes me really sad.

As soon as I could, I left my godmother's house, because I wasn't free there. They sent me to her son, to another city, Trujillo. I was working for him, but he didn't pay me, it was in exchange for a roof and food. They sent me to school, but I hardly had time, I had to do everything in the home, so I couldn't study. At least I finished high school. When I was eighteen, I met a boy, I got tough with the señor and told him I was going. They made me sign a paper saying I was going out on my own, and that if anything happened to me, they weren't responsible.

Things didn't last long with that boy, but I started working at a house. Getting paid, it was different. I didn't have to be afraid of the señora, like I was afraid of my godmother. I was at that house for three years. Another girl came, and I caught her excitement for Argentina. I told her: all right, come on, let's go. We got our passports and left. Then it was three days on a bus, crossing Chile, until we got to the capital, Buenos Aires. The little money we had ran out. We took the first jobs we could find. I was ironing clothes. One day, the man who's now my husband showed up at the hostel where we were living, he was also from Peru, and he was supposed to be just passing through Argentina on his way to Paraguay. I always tell him fate made him stop there so we would meet. I was calling him *señor*, using the formal *usted* instead of the *tú*, because he was older than me. We got engaged and went to live in a small town, San Fernando. He was working at a plastics factory. One day my mother-in-law came, mainly to meet me. I remember she told me not to get pregnant.

I did. We had no family there. I said: 'I'm going to have a child, who will help look after him.' Then, seven months pregnant, we went back to Peru and went to live with my in-laws. There was no work there, the little money we brought with us ran out, and it was all expenses, expenses, expenses. My mother-in-law was giving us food and a place to stay, but the kid needed things. There's no insurance there, like there is here. So we went to Argentina to work when my son, Fernando, Fer, was six months old. I left him with my mother-in-law and I'll never forget it. I don't like to talk about that, I always cry. I feel guilty I left him so young.

I didn't have him back with me until he was eight years old. My husband travelled every three years to see him. We couldn't go together because we would lose too much money. It was five days' travel by car. I went to see him once, when he was three, and he came to visit us when he was just five. The idea was that he would stay with us, but after two months, he just hadn't adjusted. I was working in houses and couldn't ever see him, so my mother-in-law took him back. We carried on like that, sending her money, until Argentina blew up and the banks froze. Then my husband came to Spain, with a contract a cousin had got him, and I stayed in Argentina a few more months to save up, and then I went to Peru to be with our son, who was already eight. Finally, we were like mother and son. I could take him to school, pick him up, but at first, it was hard. They had raised him right, with lots of love, especially with his being the only son of the only son, but I wanted to make my own rules, and he was already used to them, his Mamá Lucha, as he called her, and his Mamá Tita, who was his aunt. That's how it was for us for two years, living with my in-laws, until we were able to reunite with my husband in Spain. In the airport, my son started crying because he had to leave his grandmother, who had raised him all his life. It must have been hard for him too.

But my son was also excited to be with his father. We lived

in a house with the cousins. Fernando quickly adapted to school. Six months in, they told him he didn't have to go to the *aula d'acollida* anymore, where kids from other places go until they learn Catalan. My husband didn't get to enjoy much time with our son because he was doing live-in care for an older gentleman, he only saw him on weekends. I also started taking care of an older woman with Down syndrome, and we were able to get that family to rent us a flat they owned. They paid me 700 euros a month and the rent was 750, so we couldn't save much. On Saturdays and Sundays I took the señora for walks, and they paid me extra for that. What happened was, I got pregnant with my second child, and the señora didn't like it, she took away my extras.

I always knew I had to give my son a younger sibling; I couldn't leave him alone like I was, growing up without family. I wanted to, but I kept putting it off and putting it off. I was older, over forty, when I got pregnant, but I fell down some stairs and lost the baby. I thought that would be it, but two months later, I was pregnant again. I thought: 'He'll be born if he's born. But I'm not going to be taking care of myself or anything, because I can't stop working.' I was working right up until the last day, with my belly and everything. And he was born, he was born. There I was, forty-two, with a baby and an eighteen-year-old son, already off to college. He always studied so hard. He double majored in economics and statistics, with a full scholarship. Just then, the economy came crashing down. They wanted to kick us out of the flat, and I didn't want them to evict us, because I didn't want my sons to be ashamed.

I've noticed a difference in my relationship with my two sons, because I couldn't raise the first one, but this is also really, really hard. It's really hard to raise a child in Barcelona, without family. You work just to pay someone to watch your kid. And sometimes you have money but no one to show. It's a good thing he's nine now, he can be alone for a few hours at a time. I don't have friends here either, just another mum from the school, Laura, who's great. It's so hard to raise a child in Barcelona. He was always getting sick. I don't know why, but I got depressed. I've been taking medication for three years, but I'm finally coming out of it.

Sometimes I tell my children about my life, and it doesn't compare with theirs. They've been cared for, given love and hugs, and I had none of that. I was without the biggest thing, a mother's love.

Right now, we're happy, in quotation marks. I can't forgive myself for having left the older one. He says: 'Mum, don't feel bad, they took care of me.' But I always feel bad when I talk about that. I always kiss and hug the little one, and I ask him: 'Are you happy? Are you happy?' The older one too. He seems happy to me, with his girlfriend and his job. I tell him: 'Fer, you'll never be poor again.'

The Underground Conversation

While this book was taking shape, I interviewed an author a little younger than me for a magazine. She had written a strange and dazzling novel that I recommended to everyone. The conversation was nice, one of those interviews where the memory is more rewarding than the write-up. When you listen to the audio later, to transcribe it, you realise that it's too long, that you didn't go in search of the statements your article would need in order to have a good title and a through line. It has happened again, you've let yourself be carried away by how stimulating it is to have someone in front of you who, in that moment, with a coffee in her hand, seems to be there of her own free will, because she wants to be your friend, and not because of the obligations of promoting a book. Those conversations are a reward in a job that is often thankless.

At the end of the interview, when I had already stopped recording with my iPhone and we were saying goodbye to each other, the young (but not so young) and brilliant (very) writer asked me about my children, whom I had mentioned earlier. 'You can do it, right? Write and have children. Lots of people do it,' she asked, tentative. She told me she used to think she didn't want to be a mother, but lately, she had been having doubts, yet she wasn't sure how to fit together all the pieces of her life and add that in too. For several minutes, the sounds coming out of our mouths made explicit a conversation that had in fact been happening earlier, implicitly, while we were talking about her book. I'm not surprised.

Sometimes I think that all women of a child-bearing age, and by 'child-bearing age' I mean specifically among the somewhat educated middle class in the West, which is a very short span of time and runs from thirty-four to forty-two years old, spend a decade holding an underground conversation.

Even when we're not really talking about it, we're talking about it. Do you want to have a child? Do you want to have one now? Do you want to have *another* child? Can you? How exactly will you deal with the hypothetical child who will rob you of sleep and time? Do you have a good plan? Is there someone who will inseminate you? Are you going to do it with a partner, alone, or by concocting some novel social-familiar arrangement? Have you thought about how you're going to raise the child without ceasing to work, sleep, and eat?

Nor are the women who don't want children allowed to remain outside of the underground conversation, because from them, a manifesto is demanded, a response, a plan that justifies their decision not to have children. In many cases, they devote years to 'the conversation' before arriving at a committed no.

I'm aware that in my last decade of work as a journalist, I've wasted many minutes of interviews with fascinating women – women who write novels, who research rare illnesses, who design museums, who shoot movies – having some version of that conversation. Sometimes I initiate it, but on many occasions, they do, maybe because they sense that their audience is receptive, that I've been immersed in it all. Another successful essayist asked me about my children a lot when we met to discuss her book, and three months later, I found out she was pregnant. Clearly, she was in an advanced stage of the conversation.

I imagine that many of my colleagues aren't doing this, are instead investing all those minutes, which add up over the course of a decade, in continuing to discuss their subject's speculative fiction, or essays about burnout, or sustainable urbanism, accelerating climate change, cancel culture, whatever. Meanwhile, I wasted a portion of my allotted time with some of the most impressive minds of my era talking about things I could have talked about with my friends at a bar.

I usually don't feel too bad about it, really. Often, those moments are what I recall most strongly from the interviews. And other times, when I talk about my children, the interviewee opens up a bit, reveals aspects of her own life that go beyond the phrases she prepared for promoting her work, which even the most generous interviewees must resort to, because it's impossible to offer new material to every journalist who plants herself in front of you. One successful author had me on the ropes, was monosyllabic and apathetic, avoiding eye contact, until a message from his son arrived and he showed it to me. 'There comes a time when they only text you to ask you for money,' he said. The interview took a turn at that point, and the writer began to talk more like a person with foibles and less like an egocentric literary figure.

Remembering that conversation, I also think of a trivial moment backstage at a literary festival, where participants can rest before and after their events, and where there are usually a couple of tables with sandwiches and drinks. Spontaneously, small groups emerged separated by gender – that this custom persists never fails to surprise me – and the women, writers, editors, a quite famous singer, and a few culture journalists ended up (we ended up) talking about our children, real and hypothetical, while the men a few metres away discussed, I suspect, something about the agenda for the festival, or their respective podcasts, who knows.

Weren't we all supposed to be there invigorating the cultural sector? Why were we talking about 'adaptation week' at preschool? What had happened to our exhausted brains the moment we turned thirty-five? Did we really have nothing more to offer? Or was that precisely the 'more' we needed to focus on? Maybe we were finally centring the famous labour of caregiving the way the new Left has been preaching for the last decade? But if that were the case, why did we all have that same tired expression, identical violet circles under our eyes? To be honest, in that moment, we didn't seem very dynamic or re-vitalising.

Once, I asked a writer from the United States if the fact that she had a daughter had changed her perspective or even her approach to writing. It was a fashionable debate at that time. Several authors had said that having children had made their books more fragmentary, that after becoming primary caregivers, they wrote in shorter, syncopated paragraphs due to the constant interruption. The author refused to answer and told me she found the question offensive and sexist. She specifically said: 'People always ask women writers that. When you start asking the men, maybe I'll give you a real answer.'

That response annoyed me, of course. What do you know, lady, I thought. Barely two weeks before I had been talking with Richard Ford about his absolute conviction that authors should never have children. My feminist credentials are perfectly up-to-date, all my papers are in order. You can check. I've done every crash course.

Now that a few years have passed, I can see that she also had a point, and that it's unfair and reductive to drag women into the underground conversation if it legitimately doesn't interest them. But we're also deceiving ourselves if we pretend it isn't happening, if we try to deny that many women in their repro-ductive years have spent the better part of a decade struggling with the conflict of whether or not to conceive, and how. And that it deforests our neural resources, wrests the oxygen from all those other ideas we could be having. I'm interested in the motherhoods (and non-motherhoods) of my friends and the women I encounter in life, just as I'm interested in their ideas and their novels.

Some of the women who show up in these pages, my aban-doners, with whom I've had a very intimate, somewhat toxic relationship, tried to flee from the underground conversation. Very understandably, they wanted to escape the biological curse of seeing themselves defined as women and, by extension, as mothers. Nevertheless, the conversation ended up seeping in through the crevices in their work. It happened to Doris Lessing, for instance, and Mercè Rodoreda. They left their children in other countries, but their turbulent motherhoods turned up in their novels in the most fabulous, twisted ways.

I suspect that many of the abandoners in these pages were seeking the impossible: they wanted to have children without becoming mothers. I can't think of a more relatable desire.

I admit that spending months reading about them in order to write this book was a bit self-indulgent. Elizabeth Wurtzel, the late and controversial author of the generational memoir 'Prozac Nation', said to a colleague, Emily Gould, who was getting ready to write her first novel, do a lot of research, then write about yourself. That seems like good advice for writing about anything, including women who, at some point, left their children behind.

I don't know if I can round off with a clean conclusion, if I can say, for example, 'Now I understand my abandoners better.' I always understood them – how could I not have. It seems clear that Maria Montessori would have been throwing away her scientific career if she had married and set about caregiving, that Doris Lessing needed to flee Rhodesia and couldn't have built her literary life while raising three children, that Joni Mitchell had no alternative to putting her daughter up for adoption, and that sometimes the relationship between a mother and son simply has too much working against it to function, as in the cases of Muriel Spark and her son Robin, and Mercè Rodoreda and Jordi.

Things happened while this book was coming together. What happened to me personally was relatively little. Only that, to write about abandoners, I had to abandon my own children more than usual. Sneak out on weekends with my battered MacBook Pro, to take refuge in the empty homes and offices of my friends. My goal was always to rise very early and disappear before the children woke up. Since both are gifted with hyper-sensitive radars that pick up this kind of intention, I very rarely achieved it. They got out of bed, asked for breakfast, hung from my legs, and pouted. 'You always leave,' they said, with all the melodrama small children can muster, which is to say, a lot. Once I had been away from home a few hours, my own mother would send me messages: *Still not home?* No, not yet.

Although they don't resemble each other in the slightest, as babies, my two sons both learned an action which had identical intent: they would pull the charger out of my laptop, which they identified very early on as their most powerful enemy. To be able to write this in the time I stole from my other assignments, I did what so many others do: slept little. I got up at night and crossed the hallway in the dark, paying homage to

Montserrat Roig, who was born and lived for many years one block from where I live now, in a very similar flat, with a long hallway, like most of the ones in this neighbourhood.

How did she write forty books in forty-five years, as well as thousands of articles, and at the same time raise two children alone? I ask myself that every time I pass the entrance to her building and do whatever it is we atheists do instead of crossing ourselves. Her children have said that she sometimes stayed up all night writing, and when they woke up, she burnt their toast. At most, I'm capable of setting my alarm for 6.30 a.m. Eight out of ten mornings, I had barely had a coffee and turned on the computer when I heard little footsteps in the still-dark hallway, and then my little one would appear, with his full head of hair, and plans that did not include going back to sleep. I'd like to be able to say that his emergence, that small, still-warm body in Snoopy pyjamas, made me smile. But that almost never happened. Seeing him awake made me irritated and frustrated, because in that moment, it became clear that the promise of productivity in the day extending before me was already threatened, and I knew the hours of sleep I had sacrificed would be spent giving the child his bowl of rolled oats and milk.

That's a key feature of turbomotherhood: the virtuous option always requires more time and more attention than the guilt-inducing one. Sugar-free oats are more difficult to get a small child to eat than processed cereals, brown rice takes almost twice as long as white rice to cook. If you want to do it well, if you aspire to an Olympic certificate in the category of 'mother', you'll have to place more of your time, attention, and energy on the altar of motherhood. I thought about that on those mornings, sitting in front of a Word doc called 'The Abandoners', which I was no longer going to modify in the next twenty minutes, nor the next thirty or forty.

I also started seeing abandoners everywhere. In movies, in novels. The remake of Ingmar Bergman's *Scenes from a Marriage* came out and the screenwriters decided that one way to update the script was to change it so the woman left, not the man. Jessica Chastain's character, who has in her favour an extremely high salary at a tech company, goes to Israel with her new partner, leaves her daughter in Boston, and arranges an expensive means of seeing her from time to time. I responded more to Maggie Gyllenhaal's adaptation of *The Lost Daughter*, by Elena Ferrante, which premiered as I was finishing this book. I have floral-print shirts and plaid blazers like the ones Jessie Buckley wears in the movie. I haven't read Yeats, the poet she translates, but I understand what it means to make your living interpreting words that other people have written. And above all else, I know very well how it feels to live in interruption, as Leda does in the movie. Both she and Nina, the other young mother in the story, find their small daughters take ownership of their time and their actions in a very capricious way, whenever they like. Which is all the time. They interrupt their mothers' work calls, they cover their mouths with their hands when they try to talk. In one scene, the daughters approach Leda while she's trying to masturbate in front of the computer. Both Gyllenhaal and Ferrante do an excellent job conveying the idea that caring for young children is like renting out your own body.

In the movie, Leda is constantly encountering men who didn't raise their children, who even lived on another continent while their mothers raised them. Their stories are banal, common. Although I would also like to know more about those fathers.

There was a moment when all of Spain began to argue about whether or not it was acceptable for a mother to cut off contact with her children, when a local celebrity, Rocío Carrasco, daughter of the famous singer Rocío Jurado, told her story in a Telecinco docuseries. Suddenly, the conversation about what constitutes a bad mother was taking place in the mainstream. Should a mother tolerate physical abuse from her own daughter? Should she immediately forgive her? Millions of people were asking these brutal questions.

The docuseries focuses on Carrasco's abuse by her ex-husband and her own daughter. Although it educated the Spanish general public on concepts such as gaslighting and other forms of psychological abuse, its approach wasn't always elegant. While speaking with Carrasco, the producers projected giant pictures of her dead mother and absent children – Spanish lacks a word as precise and moving as the one used in English 'estranged children', children who have become strangers – centimetres away from her face as she howled in pain. The format puts us on our guard and generates maximum discomfort. As does the very commercial approach the series takes, thematically dark yet transparent in its objectives. It wasn't long before the TV channel gave space to the abusive ex-husband's second wife, which reduced any previous educational efforts to the classic chauvinistic model of the catfight. But the programme had an impact. It led many people who had never considered doing so, especially many women raised under the maternal idolatry imposed by the Francoist, national-Catholic agenda, to reflect for the first time on the limits of maternal sacrifice. As if the adage we take for granted, 'anything for the kids', was finally given some thought, on primetime TV.

This book is full of the stories of real and invented women who at some point thought maybe not everything for the kids, or not all the time. Who thought that they also needed to live and write and fall in love and become communists and stop being communists and openly experience their sexuality, and they couldn't always drag their children along those new paths with them, or didn't think it was best to.

I'm afraid I'll continue collecting stories of mothers on the edge, and monstrous mothers. Reading everything I can about Anne Sexton, who dedicated some of her most beautiful poems to her daughters, Linda and Joyce, abused them sexually, and killed herself at forty-five. About Caroline Blackwood, the aristocratic English writer and collector of illustrious husbands (Lucian Freud and Robert Lowell, among others) who was inspired by her first-born daughter, Natalya, to write a book called *The Stepdaughter*, about a fat, stupid teenager. When Natalya died two years later, at seventeen, having overdosed on heroin, even Blackwood's friends admitted that the psychological abuse and chaotic childhood her mother had given her had something to do with her very sad ending.

I'll also read, with sadness and compassion, about Jean Rhys, who left her baby on the balcony of her Paris flat while she was drinking, and was also drunk on champagne when she called the hospital to tell them the child had died of pneumonia. After that, she had another daughter, and the relationship between them was close to a catastrophe.

The pleasure and interest I take in consuming these tales of maternal disaster – with a cultural excuse – is not much different from that of the people who watched the Rocío Carrasco docuseries. When I look for information about my failed mothers, I want all the sordid details, and I want them now.

I also return to *Carol*, the story that stuck in my throat on that Sunday of wearisome hyper-mothering. In Highsmith's novel, it's clear that Carol's surrender happens in two stages. First, when Harge, Carol's odious husband, blackmails her with recordings of her conversations with her young lover Therese, she gives in. She decides not to fight for custody of her only daughter, Rindy, in exchange for the promise the husband's lawyers make her: that she'll be able to spend a few weeks a year with her. They demand that she break things off with Therese and never see another woman.

Therese understands this and at the same time it makes her feel insignificant, because her lover, her love, has chosen her daughter over her. When the two finally meet again in New York, and Therese is no longer the frightened novice she was when they met but a woman with clear ideas about her own desire, Carol tells her they're hardly letting her see her daughter one or two afternoons a year. 'I've lost completely,' she says. 'I refused to make a lot of promises he asked me to make. And the family came into it, too. I refused to live by a list of silly promises they'd made up like a list of misdemeanours – even if it did mean that they'd lock Rindy away from me as if I were an ogre.' She would almost prefer not to see the girl anymore, she admits. She says she won't even demand it. Therese deduces from all this that Carol loves her more than she loves her daughter. Which, of course, is debatable.

Highsmith based the entire plot of *Carol* on the life of an ex-lover, a society woman from Philadelphia named Virginia Kent Catherwood who lost custody of her daughter when her husband, a powerful banker, hired a detective to capture proof of her with a lover.

In the epilogue to the edition published in the eighties, the author says again:

The appeal of *The Price of Salt* was that it had a happy ending for its two main characters, or at least they were going to try to have a future together. Prior to this book, homosexuals male and female in American novels had had to pay for their deviation by cutting their wrists, drowning themselves in a swimming pool, or by switching to hetero-sexuality (so it was stated), or by collapsing – alone and miserable and shunned – into a depression equal to hell.

I also prefer to see Carol and Therese's conclusion that way, not as a happy ending, but as an attempt at happiness, a 'reasonable dose of hope', as the (too liberal) Spanish translation put it. That is aspiration enough, and also turns out to be perfectly compatible with the 'daily sadness' Ingrid Bergman talks about. I like to imagine a sequel to the novel in which Rindy shakes off at least a portion of her father's ideas, is corrupted by a certain counterculture (after all, Rindy will become an adult in the sixties), and tries to reunite with her mother, who, as a child, she must have seen as an abandoner.

Practising a kind of wishful thinking, like children do when a story ends and they ask you to keep going now that everything bad has been exorcised, I imagine that they find a way to understand each other, and that the daughter no longer expects Carol to be a mother, not in the most oppressive sense of the word. She doesn't need to be taken care of, just needs her to be there. Still imperfect, but within reach.

Acknowledgements

I suspected, and have now confirmed, that writing something long makes you a slightly worse person. A worse partner, a worse friend, and also a worse mother. The document living on your computer steals your hours and attention from people who love you. So I'll take advantage of this acknowledgements section to ask for the forgiveness of those affected, starting with the three who matter to me most. *Thank you, my dears, for everything.*

Thank you, Anna Soldevila, for your breath and your patience. Mariàngela Vilallonga, for your guidance in the hermetic Rodoredan world, and Joan Bofill for sharing your memories of Cécile Éluard.

I would not have been able to finish this without the constant support of Noelia Ramírez. I'm also indebted to Leticia Blanco and Álex Vicente, for tolerating me – and cheering me on madly – when I was frustrated, and to Miqui Otero, who gifted me an idea for a chapter at my dining-room table, like someone passing the bread. Ariana Diaz lent me a refuge when I needed it, and Aida Cabrera and Sílvia Clua always showed me their warmth. I'm also grateful to Mar García Puig for her careful read.

Thank you to my parents, for your love (and also for the books), and to my sister, co-conspirator in childhood and beyond.

Bibliography

What Kind of Mother Abandons Her Child?

Diski, Jenny, 'Entitlement', *London Review of Books*, June 2001 <https://www.lrb.co.uk/the-paper/v23/n20/jenny-diski/entitlement>.

Cook, Emma, 'Granny, Noddy and Me', *Guardian*, 13 November 2009 <https://www.theguardian.com/lifeandstyle/2009/nov/14/enid-blyton-noddy-sophie-smallwood>.

Muriel Spark: A (Male) Writer's Life

Spark, Muriel, 'The Gentle Jewesses', *The New Yorker*, June 1963.

——. *Bang, Bang You're Dead & Other Stories* (London: Granada, 1981).

——. *Curriculum Vitae: An Autobiography* (London: Lives and Letters, 1992).

——. *La plenitude de la señora Brodie* (Valencia: Editorial Pre-Textos, 2006).

Stannard, Martin, *Muriel Spark: The Biography* (London: Orion, 2010).

Sudjic, Olivia, *Exposure* (London: Peninsula Press, 2018).

Good Bad Mothers and Bad Bad Mothers

Bennett, Laura, 'The First-Person Industrial Complex', *Slate*, 14 September 2015 <https://www.slate.com/articles/life/technology/2015/09/the_first_person_industrial_complex_how_the_harrowing_personal_essay_took.html>.

Brody, J. E., 'Parenting Advice from America's Worst Mom', *New York Times*, 15 January 2015.

Chen, V., 'Why the Tiger Mom's New Book Makes You Nervous', *Time*, 31 January 2014 <https://time.com/2963/amy-chuas-new-book-might-make-you-uncomfortable-but-its-not-racist/>.

Chua, A., 'Why Chinese Mothers Are Superior', *Wall Street Journal*, 8 January 2011.

Donath, O., *Madres arrepentidas* (Barcelona: Reservoir Books, 2016).

Fischer, S., *Die Mutterglück-Lüge* (Munich: Ludwig Verlag, 2016).

Neal, M., 'Why I Left My Child', 3 October 2016 <https://neal-michon.medium.com/why-i-left-my-child-20a11ed296e6>.

Rizzuto, R., 'Why I Left My Children', *Salon*, 1 March 2011 <https://www.salon.com/2011/03/01/leaving_my_children/>.

Tolentino, J., 'The First Essay Boom is Over', *New Yorker*, 18 May 2017 <https://www.newyorker.com/culture/jia-tolentino/the-personal-essay-boom-is-over>.

Waldman, A., 'Truly, Madly, Guiltily', *New York Times*, 27 March 2005 <https://www.nytimes.com/2005/03/27/fashion/truly-madly-guiltily.html>.

Gala Dalí and the Matter of the Magnetic Woman™

Dalí, G., *La vida secreta* (Barcelona: Galaxia Gutenberg, 2013).

De Diego, E., *Querida Gala: las vidas ocultas de Gala Dalí* (Barcelona: Espasa, 2003).

Jamison, L., *Make It Scream, Make It Burn* (Minneapolis: Graywolf Press, 2019).

Montañés, J. Á., *El niño secreto de los Dalí* (Barcelona: Roca Libros, 2020).

Parker, D., *Narrativa completa* (Barcelona: Lumen, 2003).

Pérez Pons, M., 'La hijastra de Dalí reivindica su lugar', *El País*, 2017.

Poirier, A., 'Watching Boxing with Picasso and a Ménage à Trois at Home: My Life with the Surrealist Elite', *Guardian*, 12 April 2014 <https://www.theguardian.com/artanddesign/2014/apr/13/cecile-eluard-childhood-pablo-picasso>.

Zgustova, M., *La intrusa: retrato íntimo de Gala Dalí* (Barcelona: Galaxia Gutenberg, 2018).

An Ogre, a Princess, an Ass: Mothers Who Leave in Meryl Streep's Career

Carstens, L., 'Sexual Politics and Confessional Testimony in Sophie's Choice', *Twentieth Century Literature*, 47 (2001).

Cusk, R., *Despojos: Sobre el matrimonio y la separación* (Barcelona: Libros del Asteroide, 2020).

Duras, M., *La vida material* (Madrid: Alianza, 2020).

Ozick, C., 'The Rights of History and the Rights of Imagination', *Commentary*, March 1999.

Schulman, M., *Meryl Streep: Siempre ella* (Barcelona: Belacqua, 2007).

Styron, W., *La decisión de Sophie* (Barcelona: Belacqua, 2007).

Ingrid Bergman: A Daily Sadness

Bergman, I. and Burgess, A., *Ingrid Bergman: My Story* (New York: Delacorte Press, 1980).

Ingrid Bergman: In Her Own Words. Dir. S. Björkman, Rialto Pictures, 2015.

Longworth, K., 'Gossip Girls: Louella Parsons and Hedda Hopper', *You Must Remember This*, 1 July 2021 <http://www.youmustrememberthispodcast.com/episodes/2021/9/1/gossipgirl sarchive>.

Renoir, J., Thompson, D., and LoBianco, L., *Letters* (London: Faber & Faber, 1994).

Doris Lessing's Third Son

Adams, T., 'Jenny Diski on Doris Lessing: "I was the cuckoo in the nest"', *Guardian*, 7 December 2014 <https://www.theguardian.com/books/2014/dec/07/jenny-diski-doris-lessing-cuckoo-in-nest>.

Diski, J., *In Gratitude* (London: Bloomsbury, 2016).

Ellen, B., 'I have nothing in common with feminists, they never seem to think that one might enjoy men', *Guardian*, 9 September 2001 <https://www.theguardian.com/books/2001/sep/09/fiction.dorislessing>.

Feigel, L., *Free Woman: Life, Liberation and Doris Lessing* (London: Bloomsbury, 2018).

Lessing, D., *Un casamiento convencional* (Barcelona: Argos Vergara, 1980).

——. *El cuaderno dorado* (Barcelona: Debolsillo, 2021).

——. *Dentro de mí* (Under the Skin) (Barcelona: Debolsillo, 2008).

——. *Un paseo por la sombra* (Barcelona: Debolsillo, 2008).

——. *El quinto hijo* (Barcelona: Debolsillo, 2021).

——. *To Room Nineteen: Collected Stories* (London: Jonathan Cape, 1978).

Phillips, J., *The Baby on the Fire Escape: Creativity, Motherhood, and the Mind-Baby Problem* (New York: W. W. Norton & Company, 2022).

Winnicott, D., *Babies and Their Mothers* (New York: Hachette Books, 1992).

Momfluencers and the Economy of Turbomotherhood

Davey, M., *Maternidad y creación* (Barcelona: Alba, 2020).

Hays, S., *The Cultural Contradictions of Motherhood* (New Haven: Yale University Press, 1998).

Moscatello, C., 'Un-Adopted: YouTubers Myka and James Stauffer shared every step of their parenting journey, except the last', *New York Magazine*, 18 August 2020.

Piazza, J., *Under the Influence*, iHeartRadio.

Nora Helmer and Anna Karenina: Stray Creatures

Anonymous, 'Natural Mothers in Henrik Ibsen's *A Doll House*', 123HelpMe <https://www.123helpme.com/essay/Natural-Mothers-in-Henrik-Ibsens-A-Doll-355981>.

Cusk, R., *A Life's Work* (London: Faber & Faber, 2008).

Ibsen, H., *Casa de muñecas*, trans. by Juan José del Solar (Barcelona: Austral, 2010).

Morson, G. S., *Anna Karenina in Our Time* (New Haven: Yale University Press, 2011).

Popoff, A., *Sofia Tolstoi* (Barcelona: Circe, 2011).

Tolstoy, L., *Anna Karenina*, trans. by Víctor Gallego (Barcelona: Alba, 2012).

Tolstoy, S., *Diarios (1862–1919)*, trans. by Fernando Otero Macías and José Ignacio López Fernández (Barcelona: Alba, 2010).

What If?: The Braided Songs of Joni Mitchell and Vashti Bunyan

Bean, J. P., *Singing from the Floor: A History of British Folk Clubs* (London: Faber & Faber, 2014).

Fromm-Reichmann, F., 'Notes on the Development of Treatment

of Schizophrenics by Psychoanalytic Therapy', *Psychiatry: Journal for the Study of Interpersonal Processes* (Washington: William Alanson White Psychiatric Foundation, 1948), pp. 263–273.

Malka, M., *Joni Mitchell in Her Own Words* (Toronto: ECW Press, 2014).

Walker, M., *Laurel Canyon: The Inside Story of Rock-and-Roll's Legendary Neighborhood* (New York: Farrar, Strauss & Giroux, 2007).

Yaffe, D., *Reckless Daughter: A Portrait of Joni Mitchell* (New York: Sarah Crichton Books, 2017).

It's the Mother's Fault

Bettleheim, B., *The Empty Fortress: Infantile Autism and the Birth of the Self* (New York: Free Press, 1972).

Coontz, S., 'When We Hated Mom', *New York Times*, 5 August 2011.

Dolnick, E., *Madness on the Couch: Blaming the Victim in the Heyday of Psychoanalysis* (New York: Simon & Schuster, 1999).

Harnett, E., 'Married to the Momism', *Lapham's Quarterly*, 23 July 2020.

Lombrozo, T., 'Using Science to Blame Mothers', NPR, August 2014.

Maria Montessori: The Child and the Method

De Stefano, C., *El niño es el maestro. Vida de Maria Montessori* (Barcelona: Lumen, 2020).

Henny-Montessori, M., 'From the Writings of Mario Montessori's Daughter, Marilena Henny-Montessori' <https://www.amc-llc.us/montessori/mario-montessori> (Accessed: 4 March 2024).

Metzl, J., 'The New Science of Blaming Mothers', MSNBC, 16 July 2014.

Montessori, M., *Por la causa de las mujeres* (Madrid: Altamarea, 2020).

Pollack, R., *The Creation of Doctor B: A Biography of Bruno Bettelheim* (New York: Touchstone, 1998).

Richardson, S. S., 'Society: Don't Blame the Mothers', *Nature*, August 2014.

——. *The Maternal Imprint: The Contested Science of Maternal-Fetal Effects* (Chicago: The University of Chicago Press, 2021).

Stanging, E. M., Maria Montessori: Her Life and Work (London: Penguin Putnam, 1998).

Wylie, P., *Generation of Vipers* (Funks Grove, Illinois: Dalkey Archive Press, 1996).

Mercè Rodoreda: Forest Bird

Arnau, C., *Cartes de guerra i exili (1934–1960)* (Barcelona: Fundació Mercè Rodoreda, 2017).

Ibarz, M., *Rodoreda. Exili i desig* (Barcelona: Empúries, 2008).

Pessarrodona, M., *Mercè Rodoreda y su tiempo* (Barcelona: Bruguera, 2005).

Rodoreda, M., *Mirall trencat* (Barcelona: Edicions 62, 1982).

——. *La plaça del Diamant* (Barcelona: Club Editor, 2016).

——. *Cartes a l'Anna Murià (1939–1956)*, ed. by B. L. Vidal and M. Bohigas (Barcelona: Club Editor, 2021).

Rodoreda, M. and J. Sales, *Cartes completes* (Barcelona: Club Editor, 2008).

Roig, M., *Retrats Paral·lels, una antología*, ed. by Gemma Ruiz and Albert Forns (Barcelona: Edicions 62, 2019).